COARSE
FISHING

UK price £4.95

THE ANGLER'S GUIDE TO
COARSE FISHING

BILL HOWES

a Salamander book

Published by Salamander Books Limited
LONDON

A SALAMANDER BOOK

© 1985 Salamander Books Ltd.,
Salamander House,
27 Old Gloucester Street,
London WC1N 3AF,
United Kingdom.

ISBN 0 86101 154 6

Distributed in the UK by Hodder and Stoughton Services,
P.O. Box 6, Mill Road, Dunton Green,
Sevenoaks, Kent TN13 2XX.

All correspondence concerning the content of this volume should be addressed to Salamander Books Ltd.

AUTHOR

Bill Howes began his angling career as a boy, fishing in the local canal. He progressed to become a skilled all-round angler, and has caught many fine specimens of coarse, game and sea fish. He has taken part in many freshwater and sea fishing competitions, and has been a member – and twice team captain – of seven England teams competing in international sea angling events. As an angling journalist and photographer, Bill has written and illustrated hundreds of articles for the angling press, and has been the author of 15 books on fishing. A former evening-class instructor on angling techniques, he has also broadcast on radio and television.

CONSULTANT

Len Cacutt has spent 20 years closely associated with angling journalism and literature as editor of a number of publications. He was founder-editor of *Angler's Mail* and editor of *Fisherman's Handbook* and *Fisherman's Weekly*, and has acted as editor and consultant for many angling books. As an author, his own works include *The Evolution of the British Fishes* and *The Anglers' Handbook*.

ACKNOWLEDGMENTS

The author and publishers would like to thank the following for their contributions to this book: Geoff Bucknall, Frank Gutfield, Trevor Housby, Andy Love, Eric Pace, Peter Stone, Peter Wheat.

CREDITS

Editor: John Woodward
Designers: Tony Dominy, Charing Graphics Kent
Colour reproductions: Melbourne Graphics
Filmset: SX Composing Ltd.
Printed in Belgium by Henry Proost & Cie, Turnhout

CONTENTS

INTRODUCTION

Freshwater fish can be divided into two groups for angling purposes: the game fish such as salmon and trout, which are usually fished for using artificial flies or lures, and the coarse fish which are normally caught on edible baits. The term coarse has never been satisfactorily explained, since these species are neither 'coarse' (apart from their eating qualities, and even then it does not apply to all of them), nor are they found in poor, unattractive 'coarse' waters. Most of the popular coarse fish are members of the large carp family, known as the cyprinids, and range from the true carp, which can grow very large indeed, to small fish such as the gudgeon and bleak, Other coarse species valued by the angler are the predatory fish such as the pike, perch and zander.

Most waters other than those polluted by industrial effluent are able to hold a head of fish, fast mountain streams and chalkstreams being the haunt of the game fish while the slower lowland rivers are occupied mainly by the coarse species. Inevitably there are many waters where both kinds of fish can be found – chub and trout, for example, often compete for food in the same river.

Naturally the newcomer to angling will ask 'Where can I go to fish?' The answer to this depends very much on where he lives. Many countrymen know their local rivers and lakes, and the fish they contain, but the town-dweller may find the search for fishable water more difficult. In such cases he is advised to seek out his local angling club – there certainly will be one – where he will find advice both on the local fishing regulations and on how to get to the best fishable water.

The angler has to take account of the law. All water which is not tidal is owned by someone, and there are water authorities which control it. These bodies are empowered to issue rod licences, and it is essential to obtain one of these before fishing. Some waters are 'free' in that per-

mission is not needed to fish them, but never assume that this is the case. A water authority rod licence does not give the holder permission to fish, and a separate permit is usually required. The local tackle dealers may sell water authority licences for the area, and sometimes for adjoining areas; they will also advise on where to get permits for local waters.

The general close season for coarse fishing in Britain is March 15 to June 15 inclusive, but in some areas the season opens on June 1. In other areas there is no close season; fishing is allowed all the year round.

Today's fishing tackle is universal, and the holidaying angler can pack his gear when going abroad, but he should check on licences and permission, asking at travel agencies for brochures carrying this information. Some memorable angling holidays can be enjoyed abroad, fishing both for familiar species and exciting new species.

There is an unwritten code of conduct for anglers. Apart from respecting the general provisions of the Country Code, all anglers should take particular care to carry away their rubbish with them, and not leave it on the banks. Cattle have been choked to death as a result of eating plastic bags, and have badly cut their mouths on the rusty jagged edges of discarded cans. Some associations prohibit glass bottles on fisheries, broken glass being a clear danger to all. Nylon line should always be taken home and burnt, for many birds have died after trapping their legs on a loop of nylon or swallowing a short section.

Lead shot is now banned on some fisheries, because it has been held responsible for the death of swans which have swallowed it. If you use lead, always remember that it is a poison, and treat it accordingly. Take care never to spill it, and keep it in the non-spillable containers which are sold for the purpose. Better still, use the non-toxic lead substitutes which are now available from good tackle dealers.

TACKLE

RODS

The basic rod usually comes in at least two sections, joined either by a ferrule or by the top section fitting into the lower one to make a smooth joint. The butt is covered with cork rings to create a firm and warm grip, and a series of carefully spaced rod rings, plus a tip ring, channel the line so that it follows the curve of the rod, but does not touch it when playing a fish.

Once, the best rods were made of bamboo cane, split into lengthwise sections and then glued together in the form of a hexagon. This is called built-cane, and the method of construction, combined with carefully worked-out tapers from butt to tip, gave these rods remarkable resilience and strength, and an action which sets the standard for fishing rods to this day.

Cane has its drawbacks, however, the most serious being that it can deteriorate rapidly if it is not kept dry. When used harshly and for long periods a 'set' or permanent bend can become fixed so that it no longer makes a straight line. The craftsmanship involved in building rods from cane could not be copied by automation, and neither could the finishing processes which included varnishing and whipping with colourful silks to attach the rod rings.

After World War Two a period of rapid development in rod design began. Man-made materials had become available and manufacturers started searching for something that would reproduce the 'feel' and action of cane, but without its weight, cost and tendency to deteriorate.

The quest for an alternative rod-building material led first to solid fibreglass, which could be produced in tapered lengths. The colour was an attractive green and looked fine, but these rods lacked finesse when compared with built-cane, and anglers began to describe their action as like 'liquorice sticks'.

It was not long before the problem was solved. The manufacturers found that fibreglass could also be made in hollow tubes, and when they were produced in tapered lengths, with cork butts and rings whipped on, their action was a great improvement on the

Above: *The taper of the rod defines the action – the way it bends. This float fishing match rod has a through action, and bends smoothly throughout its length.*

solid glass types. A bonus was an even greater saving in weight.

Fibreglass is virtually unbreakable, totally waterproof and when made in large quantities relatively cheap. The first glass rods were manufactured in the USA, but soon other countries acquired the plant to make them and they quickly supplanted cane rods. A few anglers remained loyal to traditional cane, but since the demand had dropped off the costs rose, making rods in that material very expensive and even less attractive to the average buyer.

Hollow fibreglass rods for all fishing styles remain plentiful and very competitive in price, but as with all manufacturing and retail industries change is the name of the game. Another material has been adopted for rod-making which is even lighter than fibreglass. It is carbon fibre, yet another US invention, and in rod sections it is finer than glass and weight-for-weight much stronger. The only thing preventing it from completely supplanting fibreglass is its price, but this is slowly dropping to within the range of the average angler's pocket.

Rod styles

Freshwater fishing rods are available in a number of styles designed to meet the needs of float fishing, match fishing, legering, and spinfishing. Float rods come in lengths of up to 14ft (4.3m), enabling underarm casting to at least 28ft (8.6m), depending on the angler's skill and the immediate area of the swim. Leger rods can be shorter, varying from 9ft to 11ft (2.7-3.3m). Their taper is less acute than that of float rods, giving what is described as 'fast' action – the tip does not bend strongly, so the effect on the line is more direct for striking at long range.

Spinning rods are usually quite short, with a whippy tip action for casting artificial lures. Specialist rods run from short thin models called 'wands', used for fishing narrow streams where casting is close-range, to heavy 'feeder' rods capable of casting laden swimfeeders full of maggots or groundbait out into large, powerful rivers.

About 20 years ago, specimen hunters began designing their own rods, which needed to be capable of casting large baits a long distance, and capable of resisting the battles of powerful fish such as carp, barbel and pike, but at the same time retain the action which makes playing a strong fish so satisfying and exciting.

The first of these rods was the Mk. IV carp rod, 10ft (3m) long with a medium action all through its length. Later, a lighter version, not so powerful, appeared called the Avon. This had more 'feel' when playing a fish and at the same time had almost the same stopping power. Last came the 'stepped-up' Mk. IV, a powerful rod which could be used to cast whole herrings and other sizeable fish baits out to deep swims when pike fishing.

Another quite different kind of rod is the 'pole'. It has a very long history and used to be made of very long bamboo canes, each heavily whipped for strength, with a tip section of bone. These poles were up to 22ft (6.7m) long, and had the line attached to the tip end, no reel being used. Pole fishing has become very popular with Continental match anglers.

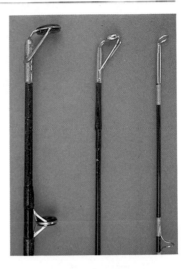

Above: *Simple rod rings are fitted to light rods (right) but the rings on heavier rods are strutted and often lined for durability (left).*

With the advent of fibreglass, poles became even more widely used, and the saving in weight was considerable. Then came carbon fibre; so light are these poles that they can be made in lengths of up to 40ft (12m).

Below: *Most pole fishermen use a pole about 20ft (6m) long. The end tackle is attached to a length of elastic fixed to the rod tip.*

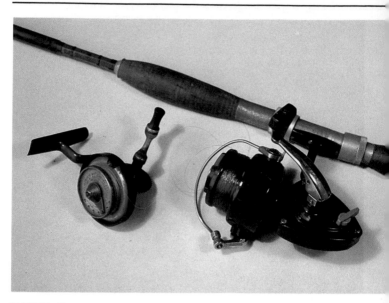

REELS

Like rods, fishing reels remain true to their past. Even the centrepin, which is little more than a simple winch with a revolving drum, still has its followers, especially those who prefer trotting the stream. This is a style of float-fishing where the bait is set just above the bottom and the current is allowed to sweep float and bait downstream. The simplicity of the centrepin allows line to flow off without hindrance.

Modern fixed-spool reels, too, are still basically the same in operation as the first ones designed by Illingworth at the turn of the century. In these reels the cylindrical spool is in line with the rod, and the line comes off the forward side. This enables casting distance to be achieved with light tackle without fear of overrun and the resulting bird's nest – a tangled mat of line which makes fishing impossible until it is sorted out.

An advantage of fixed-spool reels is that spools are available with varying capacities to suit different thicknesses of line. Obviously, the shallow spool will accept a given quantity of light line, and a deep spool the same amount of stronger, and therefore thicker line. This means that match anglers, who use light tackle, and

Above: *The fixed-spool reel is the most versatile for coarse fishing. On the left is an Illingworth No. 3, one of the earliest designs, compared with a more recent model.*

specimen hunters are able to select appropriate spools for the same model reel. These reels are also available in different sizes, making it possible to choose a small reel for fine legering using a light rod, and a larger reel for carp and pike, where the rod is correspondingly heavier.

The fixed-spool reel does have a disadvantage, however. In windy conditions, especially when the wind is blowing into the angler's face, casting can be difficult. The line tangles behind the spool, round the spindle, or over the bale-arm. The awareness of this problem led to a major improvement in fixed-spool design: the closed-face reel. This type of reel has the spool enclosed in a cover, so that loose coils of line cannot become tangled in the mechanism.

When loading a fixed-spool reel take care to fill it correctly, to within ⅛in. (3mm) of the lip. If the spool is over-filled, there will be trouble when casting, as loops of line will pull away and create bird's nests. If the reel is under-filled, casting distance and

Above: *Multiplier reels are used mainly for spinning by coarse anglers, as they have a fast retrieve rate. With practice they also permit very long casting.*

accuracy will be impaired because of the unwanted friction created as the line scrapes over the rim.

The usual method of filling a spool is to mount the reel on the rod – the butt end only is sufficient. Pass the line through the ring and under the bale arm, and fasten it to the empty spool. Take care with the knot, for it must not come loose. A line spooler can also be used. As you wind the line on to the spool keep it under constant tension by letting it run through the fingers of your free hand. Ensure that the line is wound on evenly, and does not form a hump in the middle.

Multiplier reels are basically similar to centrepins, but a gearing system is fitted between the handle and the spool so that one turn of the handle results in two or three revolutions of the spool. This gives a much faster rate of retrieve, which is useful when spinning. There is also provision for free-running of the spool and braking. These reels usually have an additional refinement in the form of a line distributor which spreads the line

evenly over the spool, a valuable safeguard when line is being retrieved quickly. A slipping clutch allows adjustment to be made so that if a fish which is being reeled in suddenly makes a lunge, the line does not break but the spool slips backwards instead.

The free-running spool makes distance casting easy, as line flows off without hindrance. But some expertise must be shown when the tackle hits the water, for the line will cease to be pulled off the drum which will continue to turn under the momentum. This is the perfect situation for a giant bird's nest! The technique of using the thumb as a brake at exactly the right moment to avoid the bird's nest has to be achieved by practice; it is not difficult, but it is vitally important.

Multipliers are very good reels for casting large lures long distances and for throwing out large baits such as herring when pike fishing.

With all reels, it is important to achieve a balance between rod and reel. It is pointless to mount a small reel which only has capacity for fine line on a rod designed to throw heavy baits, and *vice versa*. Balance is achieved when the rod is matched with a reel that carries the correct line for the kind of fishing intended.

13

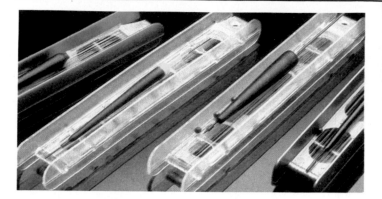

There are further moves in reel design on the way, mostly in the direction of weight saving. Extra-strong plastics and carbon fibre are being used in the manufacture of reel spools and bodies.

There are two or three methods of reel attachment. The simplest is by metal rings which slide along the cork handle of the rod. The rings are slid over the feet of the reel, lodging it into the desired position. Another kind of reel fitting is in the form of a sleeve which fits over the corks. The sleeve has a screw thread which matches threads on the rings, so the reel can be securely fixed on the rod, preventing any awkward movement while a fish is being played on the line.

LINE

Nylon monofilament is a man-made substance which many years ago replaced the old silk and flax lines, then the only medium available. Nylon is now the most popular line for coarse fishing, indeed for all sections of the sport, and for roach, rudd, bream, dace, and so on, breaking strains (b.s.) of 2lb to 6lb (0.9-2.7kg) are favoured, depending on the conditions. The breaking strain is the weight needed to fracture the line underwater. For large fish, such as pike or carp, lines of up to 12lb (5.5kg) b.s. and stronger are used.

While all nylon monofilament is manufactured by the same method of extrusion under pressure and heat there are many different brand names which are commercially available, and they vary in cost and quality in about

Above: *Line winders are convenient for storing pole fishing lines and tackle. They allow a variety of rigs to be made up in advance.*

equal proportions. The experienced angler will soon find the brand of line that best suits him and his pocket, but the beginner will be wise to select one of the well-known brands. The specialist retailer will always give good advice on line purchase, as he will on all other items of tackle.

Nylon line comes on spools holding from 25 yards (23m) to 100 yards (91m) or more. Most brands are packed in boxes of many spools which are still linked together. This enables the buyer to purchase unbroken lengths in multiples of the spool length if he wishes. Some anglers buy the smaller-capacity spools for making up hook lengths and leger links.

It is important to realise that once a knot has been tied in nylon it will adopt a permanent kink in that spot,

Below: *A simple line spooler makes reel loading easy, and keeps the line under constant tension.*

thereby creating a weak area. Short traces should only be used once, so quite a lot of nylon will be used by the angler during his fishing year.

Line winders

For pole fishing, anglers often prefer to have the terminal tackles made up ready for use. In order to keep them tidy and prevent loose line from becoming tangled with tied-on hooks, wooden or plastic line winders are employed. Each line carrying float, weight and hook is wound round a winder, all ready to go into action.

HOOKS

A bent pin with a worm impaled on it may well enable you to catch a fish, but not consistently and subtly. The modern hook as used in angling is a precision-made item and quite complex in its small way. A hook has a shank, bend, eye, point, and barb, each of which is part of a manufacturing process which at one time was done by hand. It is now accomplished by machines.

Size

The angler who wishes to fish for all the coarse species, found in very different water types and under different conditions, using the huge range of baits available, will need to be equipped with a full set of hooks of various models and sizes, ranging from the tiny No. 24 to the No. 4. The choice of hook size depends upon the bait selected which, in turn, depends on the quarry. A small hook will be needed when, as in most match fishing, large numbers of small fish are required; here a single maggot or caster is usually the bait. The hook size, in general, rises with the average size of the species to be fished for.

The hook size has of course to be matched with line breaking strain. This, in turn, must be balanced with the correct type of rod.

Hook types

The type of hook – Crystal, Kirby, straight bend, curved-in point, hollow point, long or short shank – depends on the bait, the fish sought, the casting method and the water conditions.

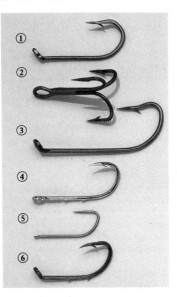

Above: *A selection of hooks:*
① *A Model Perfect, a classic design.* ② *A treble.* ③ *A long-shanked hook.* ④ *A beak hook, with a curved barb.* ⑤ *A barbless hook.* ⑥ *A baitholder.*

Some hooks are designed for particular baits. For instance, hemp can be difficult to hook, and for this a model with a flattened bend has been devised which is pressed into the split which appears during the cooking of the seed. For coarse fishermen who want to use live or dead insects, there is a hook which holds the creature without destroying its appearance.

Hooks with two barbs, called doubles, and with three barbs, called trebles, are used when attached to plugs and spinners. A modern trend is to cut one of the three barbs off a plug, both in consideration for the fish and to make unhooking less traumatic.

Never keep numbers of doubles and trebles in the same box. Somehow they always manage to become entangled into a mass of intertwined sharp points which takes a deal of time and pricked fingers to sort out.

Many anglers are beginning to prefer barbless hooks. For the matchman their attraction is the speed with which fish so hooked can be released into the keepnet – a vital matter when lots of fish are being caught. Secondly, a barbless point causes less harm to the fish, a matter which all thinking anglers should be in favour of. Lastly, they present a greater challenge to the angler's skill. When a sizeable fish is taken on a barbless hook a tight line must be kept all the time until the fish is over the rim of the landing net. One moment's lack of concentration when the fish turns, a brief second when the line slackens, and the fish is free.

Fishing with barbless hooks should be encouraged, especially if sport is to be the criterion, and not the accumulation of fish in a keepnet. The angler who can fish well in this way can really claim to be an expert.

Using hooks

The hook can be attached to the line by two methods, depending on whether the hook is manufactured with an eye at the top of the shank, or a flattened area called a spade-end. Spade-end hooks have to have the line

Below: *Most anglers keep a good range of split shot, which is used mainly for float fishing.*

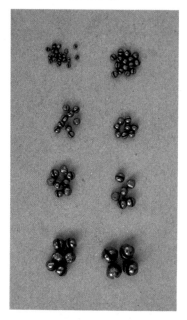

whipped on, and on a size 14 hook or smaller this needs considerable skill. Eyed hooks are more easily attached by passing the line through the eye and tying it with a special knot such as a Domhof that will not slip.

The efficiency of a hook depends on the sharpness and temper of the point. One can hone the barb of a hook to extreme sharpness, but if the metal is not properly tempered it may well snap during a fierce strike either by an angler or by a taking fish. The eye must not be capable of being pulled open as a powerful fish is being played; some anglers carefully check hook eyes and press them shut with pliers if there is any suggestion of a gap between the bend and the shank.

Hooks are the essential link between angler and fish and no effort should be spared to ensure that this vital link is not jeopardised. Never use a hook showing the faintest sign of rust. This quickly affects the strength of the metal, and the rust also gives it a rough surface which can wear line away – so check every hook before use.

WEIGHTS

In coarse fishing, weight in some form is needed for most of the techniques employed. An exception is freelining, but this method is only used by the experienced angler and demands precise control over a free-running baited hook. Unless the bait is heavy enough to cock a float or hold bottom when legered, weight is needed.

The traditional material for angling weights is soft lead, which is easily moulded to shape and very heavy in relation to its bulk. Unfortunately it is also toxic, and following allegations that British swans have been poisoned after ingesting lead shot lost in the water, it has been recommended that lead weights should be phased out. The National Anglers' Council of Britain, while protesting that the case has not been proven, is nevertheless supporting the recommendation, on the assumption that acceptable lead-free alternatives will be developed.

At least two forms of lead substitute are now commercially available. They are non-toxic mixtures which must be moulded by hand and pinched on to the line. Their efficiency seems to be equal to that of lead, but the old lead shot was simpler to manipulate.

Lead is still available, and the substitutes are not yet universally used in all sections of the sport. In consequence this section will describe the uses of traditional lead.

Shot

Split shot is squeezed on to the line in order to cock floats and also to form simple legers. It is the same shot that is used to fill the cartridges employed in 12-bore shotguns. Sizes range from the largest, SSG, of which 15 weigh an ounce (28g), to No. 8, a tiny dust shot of which some 450 weigh an ounce. The various patterns of shot placed on the line are arranged according to the depth, the buoyancy of the float, the current and the technique used.

Below: *A selection of weights:*
① *Plummet.* ② *Arlesey bomb.*
③ *Pear-shaped paternoster lead.*
④ *Capta leger lead.* ⑤ *Hillman anti-kink.* ⑥ *Bored barrel lead.*
⑦ *Bored shot on clip swivel.*
⑧ *Foldover anti-kink.* ⑨ *Bored shot.* ⑩ *Split shot.* ⑪ *Jardine spiral.* ⑫ *Trolling weight.*

Handy dispensers are available holding a selection of shot sizes, but the experienced angler will buy his shot loose in the quantity needed, keeping each size in separate non-spill containers in his tackle box.

A brand of shot manufactured for light fishing has the vivid name of 'mouse droppings' given it for obvious reasons. Those familiar with the 'evidence' of rodent activity will immediately recognise this useful little aid to the float-fisherman's art. They are made of very soft lead and are less likely to lead to false bites registered as the fish mouth them instead of the bait. They are ideal as weight when hemp fishing.

Leger weights

Legering methods are popular and highly successful angling techniques and a wide range of weights has been developed to cater for their special needs. Each has its particular use and there is a range of sizes.

The Arlesey bomb is a pear-shaped lead fitted with a swivel. It was devised for long-distance casting, and the swivel helps prevent line twist during the cast or while the weight is rolled along the bottom by the current.

Above: *Threaded on to the end tackle and secured by the hook, the plummet is used to find the depth throughout the swim, to ensure that the bait is presented properly. The*

float is adjusted until it is properly cocked in the water; neither too low (left) or too high (centre). The plummet is then removed and the hook baited up.

Some pear-shaped weights, also called paternosters, are fitted with wire loops for threading on to the line, and prevented from sliding down to the hook by shot pinched on below them. A clip swivel can be attached to the loop, and the line passed through this, allowing for a quick change of weight if necessary.

There are other weights designed to hold the bait on the bottom, even in a fast current. These have names such as 'coffin' (its name indicates its shape), and a pyramid-shaped lead complete with a built-in swivel called the Capta. This hugs the bottom, even in a current, due to the flow acting on the sides to press it down.

Spinning weights

Spinning is an active form of fishing which involves casting the lure out and retrieving continually. This is often carried out at depth and so special weights are needed both to

hold the spinner at the required depth and to prevent the line twisting with the action of the spinning vanes.

Named after its nineteenth-century inventor, the Jardine spiral lead comes in various weights and sizes and is easily attached. The line is simply wound round the spiral grooves and held in position by small wire spirals at each end.

The Wye spinning lead, again complete with swivel, is tied into the line or trace, its shape acting to prevent line twist. Other types of anti-kink or anti-twist weights are half-moons, barrel leads and Hillmans.

Plummet

The plummet lead is used to find the depth of the swim. The best is a conical-shaped lead with a strip of cork at the base and a loop at the top. The line, with hook attached, is passed through the loop and the point of the hook lodged in the cork. When

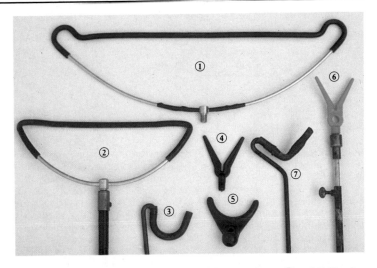

Above: *A selection of rod rests:*
① Wide rest with rubber stretched
across the fork, ideal for match
anglers in a hurry. ② A narrower
version. ③ Simple rest shaped to
hold the rod butt. ④ and ⑤ Plastic
and rubber moulded rests. ⑥ Rest
on adjustable bank stick, with a
notch to clear the line. ⑦ Simple
front rest for use with ③.

cast out, the float will not cock on the water surface if it is set too high, and it will disappear below the water if it is set too shallow. In either case an accurate adjustment of the float can be made quickly so that the bait hangs exactly where the angler wants it.

ROD RESTS

Stick a small forked branch in the ground to support a fishing rod, and you have a basic rod rest. If the branch is strong enough and the vee of the fork is smooth that is all you need. Today there are many purpose-made variations on this basic theme, and they all carry out the same function.

The all-year-round angler usually has several rod rests in pairs, since two are needed to support a rod horizontally, one for the butt and the other for the top section.

When float fishing, the front support should be wide so that picking the rod up and putting it down may be done quickly. Some models have round-section elastic suspended between the forks, an improvement on the simple vee. The rod rests should be positioned so that the rod is level, and at such a height that the angler can pick the rod up quickly when he gets a bite.

Legering needs a different rod rest technique, particularly when carp fishing. In a wind of any strength it is a good idea to position the front rest very low, with the rod top close to, or even just below the surface. This avoids much of the wind's effect on the line. The shape of the top of the front rest is important. It must have an additional indentation at the base of the vee to allow line to run freely while the rod is laying on the rest, offering no resistance to a taking fish. Carp anglers often mount an audible bite alarm on the front rest.

Sometimes bites can be registered more quickly if the rod rests are positioned to hold the rod parallel to the bankside; here, the line runs out at a right angle to the rod and a bite shows immediately as a twitch of the rod tip. This position is often used when a swingtip or quivertip rod extension is employed.

Most types of rod rest can be screwed on to a bankstick; others are moulded in rubber compound or plastic and can be pushed on to any stick of suitable length.

Above: *A rod set-up showing two types of indicator – a simple bobbin and an electronic alarm.*

Below: *A piece of folded silver paper acts like a bobbin. With the bale arm closed a pull on the line will lift the indicator.*

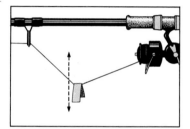

BITE INDICATORS

Anything that informs the angler that a fish has taken the bait can be described as a bite indicator, and the term is used to cover a range of devices from very simple mechanisms to electronic gadgets that buzz, whistle, bleep, flash or ring when a bite occurs.

Many commercially-made bite indicators are available. One type is a hinged lightweight metal bar which is clamped to the rod just in front of the reel. The line runs through a clip-ring at the free end, which hangs down to pull the line into a vee. If the line comes under tension the metal bar snaps level – a clear bite indication.

There are a number of electronic indicators which are attached to the rod rests, and are triggered off by the movement of the line which is placed between sensitive feelers. The alarm can be a sounder or a flashing light, and is very useful for night fishing.

The most efficent indicators for legering by day are the rod tip extensions – the swingtip, quivertip

and springtip. Most leger rods now have a special tip ring fitted that has a threaded hole at the front. The extensions can be screwed into the tip ring, and are available in various sizes.

The swingtip is a simple pliable extension which gives a sharp twitch when a fish bites. It can give false indications when the wind is blustery, however, and in these conditions the stiffer quivertip is fitted. This indicates a bite by a sudden movement at its extreme tip. The springtip is an extension which is attached to the rod by a spring.

When legering with these tip extensions the rod is set on rod rests positioned parallel to the bank, producing an angle between rod and line with the result that any bite is registered by sharp movements of the tip extension. These can be made more obvious by using a target board, which is set on the ground immediately behind the tip extension from the angler's point of view. The board is painted in clear contrasting markings so that the slightest movement of the indicator shows up.

Below: *A cork with a hair grip pushed through it makes a good indicator. Tethered to a bank stick, it flicks off during the strike.*

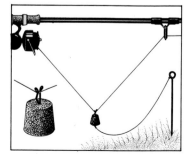

Above: *A target board of clear plastic makes the slightest movement on the swingtip obvious.*

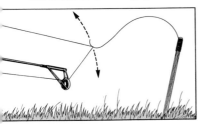

Above: *Easy to make, the spring is an extremely sensitive bite indicator. It is used mainly for swimfeeder legering.*

A useful indicator which can be made by the angler is the spring, which consists of a piece of springy wire connected to a bankstick. The free end is bent into a half-loop. When the line has been cast out, the rod is set on the rests and the spool released so that more line can be pulled off, just enough to enable it to be laid over the loop in the spring. Again the rod may be parallel to the bank, and a bite is registered as a twitch in the spring.

Bites can of course be detected by other means. The float acts as a bite indicator, and when legering the line can be held lightly between the fingers to 'feel' a bite. If calm water is watched carefully at the point where the line enters, a bite will appear as a series of radiating rings on the surface.

FLOATS

The function of a float is two-fold: to support the bait at some preset depth and to indicate by its movement whether or not a fish has taken the bait.

There are very many floats commercially available, some painted in bright, even fluorescent colours, some in dull matt black and white. Experienced anglers know that the effectiveness of a float depends on it not being obvious to the fish while being visible to the angler. It is best, therefore, for the beginner to buy a small selection based on the advice of the fishing tackle retailer, and then to find from experience which floats best suit the style of fishing and the waters in which he will pursue his sport.

At one time, floats were large quills from birds such as swans and crows, or carved from wood, cane or cork. Today, plastic forms the body of many floats, and buoyant balsa types are also in demand.

Popular designs

The *waggler* is one of the most widely used floats employed by river anglers. It does not have the traditional bulge in the body, but is slim, long and has one eye at the foot. There are sizes to suit all types of water and to fish at different depths. The body of the waggler may be sunk well down in the water, leaving just enough tip above the surface for the angler to recognise a bite. Just as its name suggests, this is registered as a distinct 'waggle'.

A *peacock quill*, from the tail feathers of that beautiful bird, is used in making various floats, and *porcupine quills* are popular, producing large, very buoyant floats.

Stick floats are another type that have no rigidly-defined shape, but they are usually long and slender. They are ideal for running water, and trotting in a light upstream wind.

The famous Hampshire Avon in southern England has given its name to a float. This strong-flowing river has long channels between weedbeds, and fishing it demands a float that will take heavy weighting and can be seen as it is carried at a pace downstream. The *Avon float* bulges at the top and is attached to the line top and bottom.

A fairly recently devised float is the **zoomer**, well named for its ability to be cast well out in rivers or stillwaters. This float is long, with the bulge well down, and it is attached to the line by short lengths of rubber tubing at top and bottom. This method of attachment is common to most floats. The zoomer is bulky enough to carry a lot of weight, which aids casting.

Balsa floats are large bodied and very buoyant floats which will carry enough shot to get the bait well down to bottom-feeding fish even in a fast-flowing river. The balsa float can also be used as a slider float, one that is attached so that it can slide freely up and down the line. During the cast the slider float will stay on the surface while the bait is taken down to as much as 25ft (7.6m). The sliding float is then halted by a stop-knot tied above it. Split-shot should not be used to stop the slider float because they do not slip through the rod rings freely during line retrieval, and any line longer than the rod cannot be recovered; this makes fishing impossible. The porcupine float can also be used as a slider.

Crow quill floats have a characteristic bend in them. They make very efficient floats and have been used for very many years. Crow quills are light and sensitive, but can be affected by wind, so they are best for very quiet stillwater fishing.

The **dart** is another sensitive float designed for accurate casting. It is mainly used on canals and slow-flowing rivers. It must be shotted to take most of the float below the surface, leaving just a very short section of the antenna visible.

A very old kind of float, which is traditionally called the **bung**, is a large fat-bodied model which is used to support the weight of a live or dead fish bait. The bung is used when pike fishing, and a smaller float, a **perch bob**, is for perch.

Below: *A selection of floats:*
① *Crow quill, fixed by a top rubber and the bottom eye.* ② *Avon.*
③ *Waggler, of the bodied type, with locking shots.* ④ *Peacock quill, with locking shots.* ⑤ *Balsa.*
⑥ *Stick float, fixed with top and bottom rubbers.* ⑦ *Dart, fished as a slider and located by a stop knot.*
⑧ *Perch bung.*

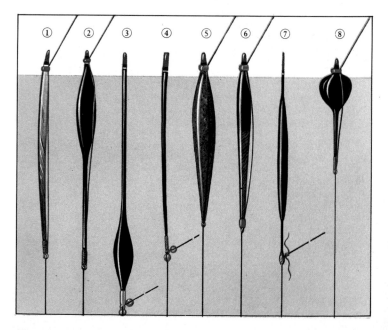

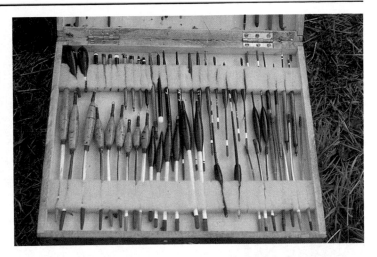

In general, the colour of floats is very important. To the beginner, those pretty red and green floats sitting in rows in the tackle shop seem attractive and 'fishy', and in the right conditions they are very effective, but under bright conditions they may practically disappear into the background. If the water is coloured – that is it is carrying a lot of suspended matter – it can appear almost black or dark brown. A red and green float might stand out well, but a white-tipped float is sometimes easier to see. White shows up well on dark water and in the shadowy reflection of foliage on the far bank.

SWIMFEEDERS

The swimfeeder is basically a lead-weighted plastic tube bored with holes, which is packed with bait particles. The baited feeder is attached to the terminal tackle in place of a leger weight. There are two basic types: the closed or blockend feeder and the open-ended feeder. The closed or blockend type is packed with maggots, casters, hemp, cloudbait or samples of whatever hookbait is in use. The tackle is cast out and as it comes to rest on the bottom water enters through the holes bored in the sides and the contents trickle out.

The open-ended swimfeeder, the same shape as the blockend, is also packed with groundbait or hookbait samples and the ends are plugged with

Above: *Delicate floats are best stored in a foam-lined box, for protection and to aid selection.*

bread groundbait which has been mixed to a consistency that will hold during the cast, but break up when the swimfeeder is resting on the bottom, releasing the contents on to the bed near the baited hook.

BAITDROPPER

This accessory may be similar to the swimfeeder in appearance, and it performs a similar task in that it deposits particle bait to attract fish to the nearby hookbait.

The dropper is a perforated container with a hinged lid, which is attached to the terminal tackle by passing the hook through a fixed ring at the top and lodging the barb in a strip of cork at the base. Maggots, casters, hempseed or other items of feed are packed into the container, the hinged lid is closed and the dropper is swung out with an easy underarm action and lowered on to the bed of the water. This method is particularly suitable in swims that have a good fishable depth.

When the dropper hits the bottom a trip mechanism operates to open the container, and the contents drop out exactly where the hookbait will be fished. The dropper is retrieved, removed and the baited hook is cast to the same spot.

CATAPULTS

Angling catapults are specially designed to shoot loose particles of feed and hookbait samples to fishing areas which cannot be reached accurately by throwing, particularly in windy weather. There are various frame designs and an assortment of pouches available, and the choice depends on the material to be thrown from them. The simple schoolboy catapult is not at all suitable. Using an efficient design, it is possible to get tight groupings of bait right into the place required, even when using small particles, and a catapult has now become an essential part of the freshwater angler's kit.

LANDING NETS

Some fish are small enough to be brought to the bank without a landing net, but when using light line anything above the 'tiddler' size should be drawn into a landing net. Large fish, of course, have to be banked this way.

Landing nets come in various types and sizes. The frame can be either round or triangular, and the latter type is preferred because of the correct method of using such a net. A fish must be drawn over the sunken rim which is not moved until the fish is safely over it, and the square front of the triangular net is the ideal shape.

The usual length of a handle is 4ft (1.2m), but there are longer versions and telescopic models double the length. Specimen hunters take no chances of losing very large fish, and they use giant-sized nets, so large they have to be reinforced by side arms nearly 3ft (1m) long. These huge landing nets can accommodate a fish weighing 50lb (23kg).

The choice of landing net depends on the species and size of fish to be caught, and the nature of the bank. An extendable handle will be necessary if the bank is high.

KEEPNETS

The modern trend is to discourage the use of keepnets unless they are necessary, such as during match fishing when the total weight of fish caught must be assessed at the end of

Above: *A proper angler's catapult with a cup pouch is an invaluable aid to efficient groundbaiting.*

the match. Here, the fish may be retained in the keepnet for as long as five hours, so the net must be capacious enough for them not to be crammed together. Another reason for using a keepnet is to hold a fish safe until a photograph can be taken, if it is a particularly good specimen or perhaps an unusual species.

A keepnet must be the biggest the angler can afford, because the health of the fish he will put in it is a prime consideration. Once, keepnets were made of a harsh cord, with large

Below: *A triangular landing net is held with the front submerged as a tench is drawn into it.*

knots. Modern nets are manufactured in a soft, knotless mesh, the finest being called micro-mesh. This helps a great deal in avoiding harm to the fish through having scales torn away and fins damaged by the abrasive action of the rough knotted netting.

Keepnets are held in position by being screwed into banksticks, metal rods with pointed ends which are pushed into the ground and positioned so that the open mouth of the net is in exactly the right place for fish to be put – not dropped – in. Telescopic banksticks are available for awkward situations.

BAIT TRAY

This is a very useful item which carries an assortment of at least four different hookbaits and holds them in just the position for rebaiting without losing concentration.

The tray is set on a metal rod, like a bankstick, and positioned by the fishing area. It carries built-in trays or bait tins, each of which is loaded with an alternative, or change bait, which can be selected in a moment.

Sometimes one part of the tray is used for holding small items of tackle that might be required quickly, such as scissors, a plummet, leger weights, a disgorger, a packet of hooks, or shot.

Another useful attribute of the bait tray is that it can be used on waters where it is necessary for the angler to wade out and stand in perhaps up to

Above: *When wading the keepnet should be within easy reach so the catch can be added without disturbing other fish in the swim.*

3ft (1m) of water while fishing. The bait tray can be positioned in shallow water close to the angler, saving him creating vibration and splashing when wading back to rebait the hook.

DISGORGERS

There are various types of disgorger, the simplest being no more than a metal rod with a notch at one end. To remove a lodged hook, the disgorger is inserted into the mouth of the fish and the notch pushed on the barb to release it. Another type is a slotted cylinder which is slid down the line, to press on the hook and release it.

Today, such disgorgers have largely been replaced by artery forceps. The forceps are gently inserted into the mouth, and the clamps lodged round the bend of the hook and locked. A gentle push forward usually releases the barb and the hook can then be withdrawn.

This accessory is especially useful when dealing with large fish and those with sharp teeth such as pike. Using the forceps keeps the fingers well away from the jaws of a pike, and even if the hook, which might be a double or treble, is well back it can sometimes be removed by inserting the forceps very carefully through the gill covers.

PLUGS, SPINNERS AND SPOONS

The showcases of tackle shops are full of brightly coloured plugs and spinners of all types, shapes, and sizes and all are designed either to wobble, spin or perform erratic movements through the water as they are retrieved. Most of them represent small fish and their actions reproduce the halting, jerky swimming movements of sick or injured fish.

Plugs are all non-spinners and their actions vary from floating or wobbling to deep-diving depending on the rate at which they are retrieved. They can be in one piece, double or triple jointed. Vanes on the flanks can sometimes be adjusted to vary the depth of dive.

Spinners and spoons are usually made of metal and come in a wide variety of shapes and colours. Most spinners are called bar-spoons, which means that the spinning blade rotates round a metal bar. These spin rapidly even at a slow rate of retrieve.

A very effective spinning lure is the Devon minnow, which has a torpedo-shaped body with large eyes painted on the front. Two adjustable vanes stick out where the pectoral fins are in living fish; these control the rate of spin. The Devon is excellent for taking pike and perch, and is also a traditional lure for sea trout.

Both plugs and spinners can be fitted to pairs of double or treble hooks. They are best carried in a partitioned box, for if left loose in a tackle box or tray they will soon get into a terrible tangle.

CARBORUNDUM

Apart from its temper, the most important feature of a hook is that it must be sharp. For this reason anglers should always carry a small carborundum stone in the tackle box. This can also be used to keep the fishing knife in good condition, for constant close proximity to water tends to dull the blade.

To sharpen a hook, hold it by the shank and gently rub the point on the stone, moving it away from the barb. Carborundum stones of just the right size and shape for angling use can be

Below: *Designed to imitate the appearance of small fish, metal lures spin, wobble and flash as they are drawn through the water, and attract predators such as pike.*

bought from the best tackle shops, but they are also available from hardware stores and tool merchants.

UMBRELLA

For anglers, the umbrella is not just for keeping the rain off, although this function is very welcome! It is also used as a windbreak, for sitting in a cold wintery wind for five hours or more can be very unpleasant.

Below: *A well-made tackle box keeps the angler's gear well-protected and in good order. The compartments have been designed to fit specific items of tackle.*

Above: *Fitted with three treble hooks, this large plug is used for trolling lakes for big pike.*

Angling umbrellas are larger and of stouter material than the standard model. The material is nearly always green, and the pole is stout, with a pointed metal end that can be stuck firmly in the ground. The best models have a tilt device in the pole. This allows the umbrella to be tilted to provide the best protection from driving rain and wind.

Some types have guy lines fitted so that the umbrella can be held stable in a strong gusty wind. A tent-cover can be used in conjunction with an umbrella, and the result is a 'brolly tent' in which anglers can sit and fish well protected from bad weather.

SUNDRIES

Among the accessories which an angler should carry in his tackle box are an old hand-towel, scissors, knife, spare float rubbers and polarised glasses. The towel keeps your hands reasonably clean and dry, especially when hunger strikes and the lunch pack has to be opened.

Scissors are essential, not only for cutting line when assembling traces, but for cutting up and removing unwanted nylon line. This must never be left on the bankside, as it can entrap the feet of birds, and even their beaks, killing them slowly and painfully.

Most anglers have a pair of polarised glasses. Their special optics enable the angler to see beneath the surface even when sunlight is glaring off the water, and they should be considered part of every angler's basic equipment.

A method of weighing fish can be carried in the form of a spring balance. The scales that include a dial and a tray usually take up too much room, but a simple spring balance occupies very little space. It is always nice to be able to verify the weight of a good fish.

If groundbait is to be mixed at the waterside – and some say that it is best to use water from the swim for this purpose instead of out of the tap – a shallow plastic mixing bowl is useful.

The groundbait mixture can be carried in the bowl during the journey to the water.

KNOTS

Every knot tied into the tackle creates pressure points on the nylon line, lowering the breaking strain and creating a weak link in the chain from reel to fish, so as far as possible keep knots to a minimum. When a big fish breaks free it is usually the knot which has failed to take the strain. Then not only will you have lost the fish, but it

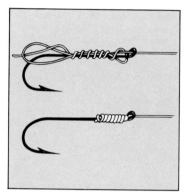

Domhof knot: *Thread the line through the hook eye (if present) and lay a loop along the shank. Whip the free end eight times round hook and line, and through the loop.*

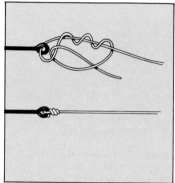

Simple eyed hook knot: *Thread the line through the eye. Twist the free end three times round the main line, up through the loop holding the hook, and back down through. Pull tight.*

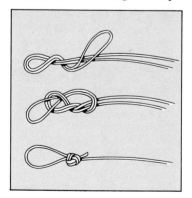

Blood bight: *A simple, strong way of forming a loop. Bend the nylon double, and twist the looped end twice round and back through. Pull tight and trim the loose end.*

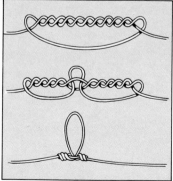

Bloodloop dropper: *Use when rigging a paternoster. Make a loop and twist the free end round the other five times. Push the loop through the centre twist.*

will be swimming about with a hook embedded in its jaw and a length of nylon trailing behind it.

Nylon is the universal material for anglers' line. It is an extremely smooth man-made fibre, and for this reason great care must be taken to tie all knots correctly, or they will slip or break. Always use the recommended knots, which have been devised to give non-slip holds.

Some anglers buy hooks ready-whipped to nylon. These generally have a loop formed in the hook link for attaching to the main reel line. The best way of doing this is to tie a loop in the main line using the blood bight knot, then join the two by passing the loop on the reel line through that on the hook link; it is then passed over the hook and the two loops are pulled tightly together.

Most anglers prefer to obtain boxes of hooks, either eyed or spade-ended, and tie them on as required. The Domhof knot is excellent for this purpose, and retains 75 per cent of the breaking strain.

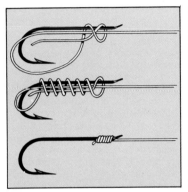

Spade end knot: *Form a loop. Take the free end, wrap it round the hook and line, and back through the wrap. Twist the loop round the hook and line five times. Pull tight.*

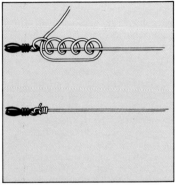

Four-turn half blood knot: *For attaching a swivel. Thread the free end through the eye and twist five times round the line, then through the loop holding the swivel. Tighten.*

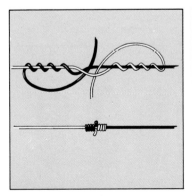

Double four-loop blood: *For joining lines of different b.s. Twist each line four times round the other, bring each free end back through the centre, pull tight and trim.*

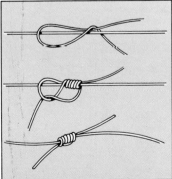

Sliding stop knot: *For locating a sliding float. Lay a short loop of nylon over the line, twist one end round six times and back through the loop. Pull tight and trim.*

BAITS

Bait preparation and presentation are among the most important elements of angling. The baits are the active components of the fisherman's equipment, and their effectiveness is crucial to success.

Maggots

There is no doubt that maggots are the most popular and widely used of all freshwater baits. They are easy to obtain or to breed, and all the freshwater fishes can be caught by using them as hookbait.

Maggots are the larvae of ordinary houseflies, bluebottles and greenbottles. Housefly maggots are called squatts. These are sold in their millions by tackledealers, often in small quantities, but sometimes in bulk. Specially treated bluebottle maggots, called gozzers, are soft and fat and as hookbait they attract more fish than do squatts. The greenbottle's eggs develop into maggots which anglers call pinkies. These small, thin 'wrigglers' have plenty of movement and are often used as loose bait to encourage fish to begin feeding. Then the angler uses the larger squatts for hookbait.

Until recently, maggots were sold in various colours – red, yellow, even bronze and green. But the colouring matter used to give them a red tint is now suspected of being responsible for skin disease, and retailers are beginning to be reluctant to sell any other than uncoloured maggots. Dyes

Above: *Mealworms need no preparation, and make a useful change bait on a slow day. They should be hooked through the middle.*

can still be obtained, but it is recommended that red colouring agents, such as Chrysiodine R, should not be handled at all.

Despite their small size, maggots are able to attract the biggest of fish, and even on a very small hook a single squatt has been known to catch pike and carp. When big fish are hooked, of course, the problem is to land them on the fine line used in conjunction with small hooks. This is where the skill of the angler is tested!

Because maggots are livebait, they have to be hooked carefully so that their 'wriggle' is maintained to attract fish. The correct way to hook a maggot is to nick the fine point of the barb into the blunt end of the maggot where two dark spots (they are not eyes) can be seen. When hooked lightly at this end the maggot will retain plenty of movement to tempt fish.

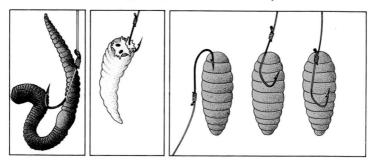

Above: *Good presentation of hookbait is essential. A large lobworm (left) should be hooked twice, making sure the ends are free to wriggle. A maggot (centre) is best* nicked with a hook in the broad end. To bait up with a single caster (right) insert a small hook through the end, work it round, then push it right into the bait, out of sight.

Single maggots act best on small hooks but as hook size is increased maggots can be attached in bunches of up to five, or even more.

Casters

The next stage in the fly's life cycle is the chrysalis, known as a caster to anglers. These are very attractive to fish and can be used either as hookbait or as loose feed.

For some reason, a can full of casters contains some that float and some that sink. The floaters can be discarded because if they are thrown in the water they will lie on the surface and be carried downstream, probably taking the fish with them. The sinkers are kept and used as groundbait or on the hook in the same way as maggots.

Given a few warm days a tin of live maggots will turn into casters, so it is not necessary to buy them. Make sure, however, to inspect the tin at regular intervals to remove any dead maggots.

Above: _Casters are easily obtained and an effective hookbait. They are also useful for mixing into groundbait, or for loose feed._

Worms

The worm has been known as a lively and successful bait for centuries. Anglers use three species of worm. By far the most popular is the garden, or lobworm; second is the redworm and third the brandling, which is similar to the redworm but distinguishable by yellow rings round the body.

The lobworm grows quite large – it can be up to 8in. (20cm) long and over ¼in. (6mm) in diameter. It can be used whole, hooked double or single, and will attract better-than-average barbel, chub, bream, perch, eels and even zander. Tench can be lured to

Above: _Maggots may be fished in the natural state or dyed various colours. Yellow maggots are dyed with annato, used to colour butter._

just the flattened tail-end, and small perch will hurl themselves at pieces of worm on a small hook.

To collect lobworms, search grassy areas in the early morning, or even at night by the aid of a torch. Your chances are improved if there has been a heavy downpour just before dawn.

A well-tried method of ensuring a supply of worms is to leave a large wet sack on the grass for a few days. Make sure it is kept moist, and when it is lifted there are sure to be a number of worms on the surface. Speed in collecting them is essential for once exposed, they will slither back down below ground very fast.

Not as large as the lobworm, the redworm reaches perhaps 4in. long. It lives in compost heaps and among rotting vegetation, so your garden may well hold plenty of hookbait.

The brandling is very similar to the redworm but the yellowish rings make it easy to pick out. It is found in compost-heaps and under the bark of fallen trees. Since both the redworm and the brandling are smaller and lighter than the lob they make excellent baits for float-fishing.

All worms can be fished whole, hooked once or twice in the middle to allow the head and tail to wriggle attractively. A limp and lifeless worm may well be ignored, even by feeding fish, but it is a rare fish which can resist the sight and smell of a juicy, writhing worm in front of its nose. When using the tail of a lobworm, insert the hook-point through the broken end, and be sure to leave enough tail to wriggle.

31

Bloodworm

Bloodworms are the larvae of Chironomids, members of the midge family that live in the mud of semi-polluted lakes and quiet waters. The adult midges swarm over water and muddy areas on summer evenings. The bloodworm – it is not a true worm – is bright red and makes a tiny bait, but it has scored big successes particularly in match-fishing on hard-fished waters, where the usual baits fail to bring results.

This bait is expensive to buy, which is understandable considering the messy business involved in collecting it. To obtain your own bloodworms, you will have to wade in thick mud and scrape the minute larvae off the surface, transferring them to a container of sieved garden peat. The bait is sometimes available in tackleshops, but do not rely on being able to buy it whenever you want.

Hooking bloodworms is a tricky operation. You must use fine-wire hooks, size 20 or 22. Lay the larva along the thumbnail and gently impale it on the tiny barb. When you have acquired the knack all the effort put in will be amply rewarded, for this is a very fine bait.

Bread

Bread can be used as a bait in several forms, and for most species of freshwater fish. The outside of a loaf provides cubes of crust; flake is the white crumb of new bread, and breadpaste is the crustless bread moistened and moulded.

Above: *Bread crust is always a good bait. The bread must be fresh, however, or it will fall off the hook during casting.*

Above: *Bread flake is simply pinched on to the hook, taking care to preserve its texture.*

To use flake, take a pinch from the spongy crumb of a fresh loaf and squeeze it directly on to the hook. The flake is best left ragged and looking natural, and is ideal for float-fishing a moving bait downstream.

Crust is obtained by cutting off a large slice of the brown outer portion, leaving a little of the crumb attached. Cut this into small bait-sized pieces in the shape of cubes. Make sure to insert the point of the hook into the crust, bringing it out through the soft crumb. Crust cubes must be kept fresh or they will crumble and fall off the hook.

The air in crust gives the bait considerable buoyancy, and this can be counterbalanced by pinching small shot on the line just above the hook.

Paste is made by cutting the crust from thick slices of bread, placing the slices in a clean towel or piece of cloth, and soaking the bundle in water. When it is saturated, squeeze out all surplus water and knead the bread, still in the cloth, to the required consistency. If you mix in crushed hempseed it makes a paste that is attractive to barbel and sometimes bream. Paste is moulded on to the hook, covering the shank but leaving the point exposed.

When fishing fairly swift streamy water the paste should be made fairly stiff so that it remains on the hook; a soft paste is best in slow or stillwater, and when only short-distance casting is required to reach the swim.

A balanced bait of paste and crust is often used by carp anglers, especially on lakes where the bottom is covered by a layer of soft weed or silt. After trial and error, the correct proportions of paste and crust are placed on the hook so that it sinks very slowly and comes to rest on top of the soft matter.

Hempseed

Hempseed is a most successful bait, although it has had a chequered history, having been accused of drugging fish and also of being too successful! Anglers fishing for roach, dace and barbel find hempseed a particularly effective bait.

To prepare hemp, soak as much of the seed as you need for the day's fishing in cold water overnight, and if necessary add a little more water to cover the seed in the morning. Bring to boiling point, and then allow it to simmer until the seeds begin to split. When this occurs, the white kernel starts to protrude from the cooked seed. It is this kernel to which the fish are attracted, and one school of thought recommends that the shank of the hook should be painted white too, to add to the effect.

There is no truth in the suggestion that hemp releases a drug into the water, thereby affecting fish. Any narcotic element in the plant does not form in the seed, which is the only part used by anglers.

Tares

Tares are cooked in much the same way as hempseed. They should then be tested to see if they are soft enough by squeezing one between finger and thumb. When ready, wash them in warm water, not cold because it tends to make them split. When the tares have cooled naturally they can be deep-frozen for future use.

This seed is used in conjunction with hemp, and very often summer roach cannot resist either of the baits. Use tares as the hookbait and hemp for loose feeding into the swim – but be very sparing with the hemp.

Wheat

Stewed wheat grains are another first-class bait, especially for big roach. One simple method of preparing wheat for bait is to first wash the grain, then put it in a saucepan, cover it with water and bring to the boil. Simmer gently until the grains start to split, then the wheat is ready for use. At this point the grains will have swollen and turned a golden-brown colour.

When baiting up, insert the hook through the protruding kernel, allowing the point to remain exposed. This increases your chance of hooking a taking fish. For its size, wheat is rather heavy and sinks fairly quickly, which is an advantage for it avoids the small surface-feeding fish and reaches the bigger specimen fish lying deep in the swim.

Below: *Uncooked tares can be crushed and mixed into groundbait. Cooked, they are a very good hookbait for roach.*

Most cereals make good baits and others worth trying are pearl barley, rice, and pasta in its several forms.

Sweetcorn

This is a fashionable bait simply because it is successful, especially in summer stillwaters. It will account for roach, chub, tench, bream, barbel, carp and other species. Sweetcorn can be bought on the cob and cooked like wheat, or it can be purchased in tins. In this form it is ready for use – but remember to have a can-opener with you in your tacklebox.

As bait, corn can be used singly or in twos and threes on the hook, depending on hook size. It can be float-fished or legered, and presentation depends on whether the species sought are surface, midwater or bottom feeders.

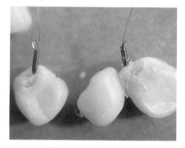

Above: *Sweetcorn is an effective bait for stillwaters and rivers. A single grain is best presented on a size 16 hook.*

Peas and beans

Fish will sometimes take garden peas fished on float tackle. When they are available, fresh peas can be removed from the pod and used as they are or lightly cooked. Tinned peas are more convenient, as are dried or deep-frozen peas , but the latter two will need cooking before being used.

Beans, such as the haricot, butter beans, black-eyed beans, broad beans or runner beans may all be used, after being boiled until soft enough to be hooked properly. Another variety which can be used without preparation are baked beans. With all these baits, appropriate hook size is important.

Above: *Green peas can be fished singly on a size 16 hook, or double on a larger size 14.*

Trout pellets

On fish farms, where trout are bred for release into fisheries or sold to the restaurant business, the trout are reared on high-protein pellets. Since they are highly nutritious they make excellent hook and groundbait for most species of fish. But the pellets are hard, making hooking difficult, and a large proportion of them float, so for bait they must be soaked and mixed with breadcrumbs, especially brown bread, or sausage rusk.

Cheese

This is not a natural bait, but like bread in one form or another it has led to the capture of many specimen fish, particularly chub and barbel. Cheese is a convenient bait which can be used without prior preparation and takes fish at any time of the year. In winter, very cold water tends to harden cheese hookbaits, which are usually employed as leger or laying-on baits.

Most types of cheese can be used, cut into small cubes, moulded into a paste, or grated and mixed with breadcrumb into a paste. The strongly-flavoured blue cheeses make good baits for use when the water is coloured and fish must find their food by their sense of smell.

Potato

Par-boiled potatoes have for many years been a proven carp bait. For carp anglers, the main advantage of the potato over most other baits is that it is seldom taken by other fish. Potato is also heavy enough to be cast well out without the need for leger weights.

Select small potatoes, about walnut size, put them into a saucepan and boil until fairly soft. They should be firm enough to stay on the hook when casting. Use a fork to test if they are cooked properly. Remember, however, that although still in their jackets the potatoes can be ruined by repeated piercing, so use just one potato for your fork tests.

To mount the potato on the hook, thread the line through it using a baiting needle. Then a large carp hook can be tied on to the line and the bait pushed down on to the bend of the hook. At this stage peel the potato, and the bait is ready for use.

Fruit baits

Elderberries are possibly the best of the fruit baits. The reason is not clear but it may be because the fruit naturally falls into the water while other fruits do not. This bait is often used in conjunction with hempseed and casters. One or two berries are set on the hook, with a few thrown in as groundbait. Take care not to throw too many in, just sufficient to attract fish into the swim. Elderberries are of course a seasonal bait, but they can be preserved for use at any time of year.

Redcurrants and blackberries also make useful baits, but they must be ripe and soft. They are used in the same way as elderberries.

Pieces of banana can be used to try for chub, carp and tench. A firm banana can easily be cut into sizeable chunks or slices and mounted directly on to the hook. With round slices a largish hook is necessary and the barb must be pushed into the centre of the fruit; make a gentle swing cast to avoid flicking the soft bait off the hook.

Above: *Elderberries are generally used as a float fishing bait, often fished with hempseed for roach.*

You will be able to recognise ripe bananas by their skins, which carry a lot of black. Their flesh is too soft to go on a hook, so again mix it with breadcrumb to produce an attractive banana-flavoured paste, very likely to entice hungry fish.

Above: *Blackberries are a seasonal bait best used for float fishing. They are particularly effective when used for chub.*

Special baits

Various recipes for many of these 'secret' baits are jealously guarded by the anglers who concoct them, and who swear by them. They are intriguing mixtures of high protein (HP) and high nutritive value (HNV) substances moulded into soft paste and hard forms.

When mixed, an HP/HNV bait can be used on the hook as a soft paste. To make hard baits (known as 'boilies') from the same ingredients, which are virtually immune to the attentions of small nuisance fish, a quantity of the prepared paste is kneaded to the required shape and size, lightly coated with a dry mix and boiled in water for a couple of minutes.

Tackle dealers and specialist bait suppliers sell packets of various bait mixes. But ordinary grocers and supermarkets also sell a wide range of flavourings, essences, colourings and additives which can be added to a base mix to produce a 'something different' recipe of HP/HNV type. And who knows, you may stumble upon a bait which always catches fish!

Ready-made boilies are available commercially for those anglers not wanting to go to the trouble of mixing their own, and these are probably the best choice for beginners using HP/HNV baits.

Above: *Crayfish are best used whole when fishing for big chub or barbel, hooked in the tail so they are still able to move.*

Crayfish

The crayfish is a valuable natural food for chub, barbel, perch and pike – all of which find this lobster-like crustacean very appetising. Obviously, then, the crayfish must make a worthwhile bait for those species. It is best hooked in the tail, which allows the animal to jerk about naturally. The average size of crayfish is between 3 and 5in. (7-13cm) and the hook size must be matched to the animal. Both live and dead crayfish are capable of attracting fish.

Crayfish have to be collected, and one of the most effective methods is to use a drop-net baited with a piece of fish. They are mainly nocturnal feeders, so the baited net is best placed in position at dusk. A line of baited drop-nets should be inspected every hour or so. Raise each net quickly, before the crayfish can scuttle away.

Freshwater shrimp

The freshwater shrimp is another crustacean which all fish eat in large numbers. They rarely reach an inch (25mm) long, and spend much of their lives among weeds or moving about on the bottom while feeding on microscopic waterlife. By using a fine-mesh net they can be collected as required, and are a very good livebait.

When baiting up with shrimp take hold of the tiny animal between the fingers and gently insert the point of a small, very sharp hook into the hard shell of its back. One or two shrimps may be used together on the hook and they work best float-fished along the fringes of a weedbed.

Wasp grub

Wasp grubs are a soft bait and so must be treated carefully. They are mainly used by chub anglers, because other species are for some reason not attracted to them in the same manner.

It takes nerve to raid a wasp nest and take away lumps of nest holding the grubs, so most anglers play safe and purchase them from bait dealers who are able to obtain supplies.

Freshwater mussel

This is a bivalve which lives in many kinds of freshwater. The larger swan mussels make fine baits for tench, but other fish species will also fall to this very tasty food.

To obtain the bait, use a strong knife to prise open the two shells and extract the fleshy 'foot' of the mussel. This has a firm consistency and will stay on the hook.

Above: *Small deadbait may be fished on snap-tackle for pike, perch or zander, legered on the bottom of the swim.*

Baitfish

Small fish may be used as livebait or deadbait for pike, perch, zander or chub. The best species are minnows, bleak, gudgeon, loach, dace, small roach and rudd, but any small fish will do. Those with flashy, silvery bodies are the most attractive.

Fish which shoal in large numbers, such as minnows, can be caught in traps. Others are best obtained by rod and line, using single maggots on tiny hooks, fished with light tackle using float-fishing methods.

Any of the above-mentioned fish are suitable as deadbaits, but sea fish such as mackerel, herring, and sprats can also be used in freshwater.

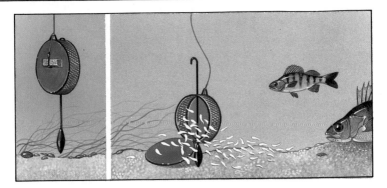

GROUNDBAIT

For most kinds of angling, success depends upon groundbaiting to attract fish into the swim. This means introducing small particles of food into the area where you are fishing, using an angler's catapult, a baitdropper, or swimfeeder. There are three forms of groundbait: balls of compacted material, loose items of hookbait, and fine cloudbait.

The basis of most groundbait mixtures is brown or white bread. To prepare it, start by soaking lumps of hard or stale bread in water until it is soft. Then drain off as much water as possible and pulp the bread by hand, at the same time mixing in other ingredients such as bran, chicken meal, and boiled or mashed potatoes.

It is a good idea to include in your groundbait mix samples of the hookbait such as maggots, casters, sweetcorn and hempseed, and if you intend to fish with worms these should be chopped up before being mixed in. Be careful not to put too many samples of your hookbait in because the fish may find so much to eat that they become overfed and ignore the bait on the hook.

A really good mixture is composed of crushed casters or hempseed, with cereal to bind it. This creates handy-sized balls of groundbait which look like currant pudding.

The balls of groundbait are usually lobbed into the river well upstream in strongly flowing water, and for this tennis-ball sized lumps are best. As they sink and break up on the bottom the particles will trickle through the swim, attracting fish to the hookbait.

Above: *The baitdropper is attached by threading the hook through the loop and lodging it in the cork. When the trip touches bottom the lid opens to release the bait.*

When float-fishing, cast upstream too, and as the flow carries the tackle down, the hookbait follows the same path as the particles of groundbait.

Sometimes, groundbait is composed of loose hookbait particles, such as maggots, which are thrown directly into the swim. Be careful not to use too much for fear of overfeeding the fish.

If you are using potato as hookbait, the swim can be groundbaited with small par-boiled potatoes. Another method is to boil them until soft, then mash and mix them with bran or breadcrumb to bind the mixture.

Cloudbait can be bought from tackleshops ready for use, but it can also be made at home to suit personal requirements. Cut a loaf into thick slices and let them dry out. Crush them and grind into a powder, using a sieve to remove large pieces. This can be taken with you to the waterside where it is dampened and squeezed into small balls which hold together sufficiently to be thrown into the swim. When they hit the water they break up immediately and a cloud of tiny particles will glide through the swim to attract fish.

Groundbait additives in the form of yellow custard powder, crushed hemp, trout pellets, sausage rusk, cheese and catfood will give taste, smell and colour to your groundbait. Don't hesitate to experiment.

WATERS

Unless they are polluted, or netted thoroughly and frequently, all running and enclosed waters will eventually hold a head of fish. They get there as fish eggs carried on the legs of wading birds, or by simple migration of fish in rivers. Small feeder streams, running into lakes, will carry fry into new areas where they become adult and breed.

The fish species will vary depending on whether the water is still or flowing, and whether it is a cold, fast-flowing mountain stream, the quiet reaches of a lowland river meandering through flat country, or the open, brackish expanse of an estuary. The game fishes such as salmon and trout and their relatives inhabit fast, well-oxygenated rivers, whereas the carp and its relatives – and indeed most of the coarse species – inhabit slower, murkier waters. Pike, chub and dace live side by side with the game fishes, but are equally at home in slow-flowing rivers. Perch can be found in almost all kinds of flowing and still waters.

In general the owner of a fishery can manipulate it to hold the species he wants to catch in the pursuit of his sport. Careful fishery management can maintain those species, but without the constant attention needed, some species will disappear, some will be reduced to a few large solitary specimens, and others, such as the rudd, can multiply so fast that the whole population is composed of small, stunted adults.

RIVERS

Rivers and streams form a large proportion of the water fished by anglers, and they hold a wide variety of fish. Bream, carp, roach, pike, perch and the smaller species are found in the slower areas, while barbel, chub, dace, grayling and the game fishes occupy the fast waters. There is also some interchange where waters of different types meet.

Where the river is rich in weeds such as starwort, crowfoot and ribbonweed, the fish are usually fat and well fed. Insects, shrimps and other small creatures on which the fish feed live among the weed and the

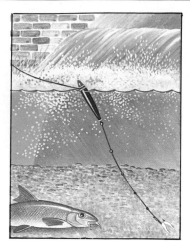

Above: *Fishing float tackle for barbel in the slacker water at the tail of the weir stream can be a useful tactic. It is essential to keep a tight line between the rod and the float in such waters. A float of the Avon type is a good choice.*

weedbeds also make ideal spawning sites for a wide variety of fish.

In the fast scours and channels between thick weeds the dace and grayling are found, while tucked under the weeds, particularly under the long fronds of ribbonweed, will be barbel and chub. These wary fish may only be seen when they emerge to feed, popping out to intercept a tasty morsel that has come down with the current form higher upstream.

A deep channel close to a reed or rush-fringed bank, perhaps shadowed with overhanging willows and alders, will always hold fish. Perch and the occasional pike lurk in the margins along the edge of the rushes and in the submerged roots of bankside trees.

Weirpools

Most rivers have a variety of swims, or sections that suit different species. Weirpools, for example, are places favoured particularly by barbel; they are found close to the weir-sill under the cascade of white water. Barbel also haunt the well-aerated water flowing through the pool, where they hug the gravelly bottom, their low-slung jaws and powerful bodies using the flow to hold them down. Big chub also prefer fast water where they snap up food items swept round in the eddies.

Weirpools always hold a wide variety of fishes, for there are swims to suit them all – turbulent water, eddies, fast runs, slacks, deeps and shallows. A weirpool offers all-year-round fishing, but it is best in the summer months because the water is better oxygenated. The tail of the weir is a particularly good fishing area. Here, different streams and currents from the weir converge, and the bottom is shallower and clean. Fish can rest without effort and feed on the matter gently swirling about.

Below: *This weir on a big river offers the angler a variety of swims, including fast waters best fished by legering, and eddies and slacks which suit float tackle.*

Where the strength of flow eases and the river widens out over shallows at the downstream end of the pool the conditions are ideal for chub, dace and barbel. When they are feeding, the perch and pike come hunting here, knowing that the small fish they prey upon will be present.

Pools and deeps

A steady flow over a deepish pool will sometimes attract and hold a shoal of roach, and a few chub may be spotted hovering just below the surface. Barbel can be expected on the beds of these pools so long as there is some flow over them.

Fairly deep, broad rivers with a steady flow of water are generally noted for bream. The fish may be found almost anywhere on the middle reaches where there are deep holes, and also in large bays.

Smaller rivers, which flow steadily throughout most of the year, often have deep holes close to the bank which have been scoured by winter torrents. These places can hold many species, including perch and pike.

Roach prefer deepish waters, not too fast, with a gravelly bed and weedbeds near by. Slow eddies and laybys, off the main flow, also attract roach. In all these quiet areas the angler's approach must be one of great caution. At the first sign of any unnatural movement the quiet backwaters will empty of fish.

Above: *Bridge supports constrict the flow of water, creating a combination of fast runs, eddies and pools holding a variety of fish.*

Bridge swims

Bridges create swims that will hold a variety of fish. The bridge supports constrict the flow of water, causing the current to speed up. This creates sheltered eddies on the downstream side where perch and pike lie. At the lower end of the faster flow, other species such as chub, barbel, bleak and gudgeon can be found.

Obviously, bridges are also very useful access points, enabling sections of bank to be fished which would be unreachable without some means of crossing the river. But those swims within the immediate vicinity of the bridge are always well-fished – because many anglers are reluctant to walk too far! You may find that it pays to walk about a mile from the access point to find a quieter swim.

Bends

The slower waters of a river on the inside of a bend are often found to harbour bream, tench, barbel, a shoal of roach and perhaps the smaller species such as gudgeon. In the faster water on the outside of the bend, where over the years the flow has scoured a cavern under the bank, swim chub, barbel, dace and roach, keeping out of the main flow.

Seasonal change

Swims that hold certain species in the summer may completely change their character in the cold months. The flow often increases, and the summer weed growth dies off because of the drop in temperature. Different swims are formed and other fish move in.

In times of flood, after heavy, prolonged rain or the melting of heavy snowfalls, fish are put off their feed for a while. But eventually hunger causes them to become active and they make their way into sheltered swims, quiet laybys, lock cuttings and even into the flooded fields. Here they can find rich pickings among the insects and worms.

Streams

You must move with caution along the bank of a stream, for the clumping of boots will certainly scare off all the fish in the vicinity. Also, when walking along a bank, keep as far from the edge as possible. Even if you do not create vibrations your shadow on the water will be enough to put the fish down. The clear, shallow waters of a stream can give the impression of looking into an aquarium. The fish can be seen – and the fish can see the angler. All movements should therefore be slowed down to avoid scaring the

Below: *Weir streams and the upper reaches of rivers are often well-oxygenated, and hold plenty of fish – particularly during the summer.*

Above: *Confluences, between small rivers in particular, greatly increase the area of fishable water, and may have a variety of swims.*

quarry. Try to keep below the horizon, whatever it is – whether bushes, trees or a raised bank.

When specimen hunting on these smaller waters the wily angler always creeps stealthily along the bank, taking advantage of all available cover. Once a fish has been spotted it is advisable to keep well upstream and work the tackle down to it.

Streams invariably have a lively flow, with clear channels between weeds where chub, dace and grayling can be found. Overhanging willows often have a small shoal of chub in residence, and these fish especially need a very cautious approach if the angler is to hook one.

Confluences

A confluence is a meeting of waters where two rivers join, or where a feeder stream enters a lake or the main river. At most confluences there is a wide area, or pool, of fishable water.

Weed growth may be present where there are eddies or slacks. These are likely places to hold fish.

An inflow from a cannery or a milk-bottling yard will offer rich feed for shoals of fish, which may include quality roach. To catch these fish in such swims you must offer them suitable baits, related to the diet they have become accustomed to.

Tidal reaches

The lower reaches of tidal rivers will hold a few saltwater estuarial species in addition to the coarse fishes. In the lower part of the estuary there will be mainly bass, mullet, eels and flounders, the last species being able to travel many miles upstream into freshwater.

Of the coarse fish, it is the dace and roach that are considered to do best in the tidal freshwater reaches. On some rivers these fish are to be found in quite large shoals and usually in swims about a rod's length out.

Sport in these waters can depend on the flow. Some rivers fish best on the outgoing tide, while others are better when the water is rising.

Above: *Tidal rivers offer good sport, for they often contain sea fish such as flounders and mullet as well as familiar coarse species.*

CANALS

Most canals offer excellent fishing opportunities, but they also vary considerably when it comes to fishable areas. Some have many miles in regular navigable use, while others are closed to traffic, abandoned and choked with weeds and vegetation. Lock gates may be broken and rotting, the banks unkempt and falling in.

Yet even these dying canals may still retain a few deep pools populated with roach, tench and so on. In some cases anglers have kept miles of canal open and fishable by constant weed clearing. Clubs that have acquired the canal fishing rights often organise working parties to clear weeds and obstructions, repair banks and piles, and create productive swims.

Sections of some canals may be featureless, with little aquatic plant growth. Finding a swim in these areas is not easy and it is often done on a trial and error basis. Plumbing the depth is always useful here and by this means the angler may find a hole inhabited by some good fish. A small bed of waterlilies or a patch of weeds may offer an indication of a roach swim.

Originally all canals had a deepish centre channel and a shallower shelf by each bank. On navigable canals weeds and rushes grow on these shelves and a gap in the vegetation could well be a productive swim. Along the edge of the shelf the roach and tench may be rooting about, while pike and big perch patrol along the edge of the weeds. Bream generally shoal in the middle where it is deeper.

Occasionally there will be other species in some places, such as gudgeon and eels. These fish seek patches of hard gravel over which they forage. Where there is a more luxuriant weed growth you may find carp and chub.

The time spent fish watching is always worthwhile, for even though the fish themselves may not be seen, bream, tench and carp send up groups of small bubbles while they root about in the silt looking for edible items.

Above: *Lock cuttings are popular with beginners, but permission may be needed if the canal is in use.*

Pike and perch often disclose their presence when small fry scatter in all directions across the surface as one of the predators lunges towards them.

Perch are to be found in the vicinity of locks, either in shoals of small fish or solitary specimens. Wooden lock gates and rotting piles are well worth fishing near if you are seeking perch.

On some canals there are places near wharves and locks where the water is extra-wide. These areas are called pounds, and they were cut to allow barges to pass, or to moor without blocking the canal. The activities of people there meant that fish came to know the areas as possible feeding places, and they can be well worth investigating.

There will also be swims worth fishing near locks where boats still go through, for the movement of the water as the lock gates open and close stirs up food and attracts fish. Because of the increasing number of holiday craft using the canal waterways more sections are kept open, and the channels are not allowed to become choked with weed. These sections become stirred up, making it difficult to see the fish.

The roving angler may come across a rotting hulk, which is another very likely place to find fish. These quiet places have to be approached with great caution if the fish are not to be

Below: *A working canal has a deep navigation channel which attracts larger fish such as bream, while the shallow shelves either side are favoured by roach and tench.*

Roach Perch Bream Tench

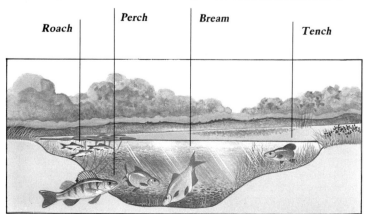

Above: *Where a feeder river joins a canal the influx of fresh water introduces food items and excavates holes in the bed, which become centres of interest for fish.*

disturbed, and the angler should keep as far away from the swim as possible. In general, though, fishing on canals is close-range work, and float tackle is better than leger rigs.

LAKES

It is not possible to learn everything about a lake on your first visit. Each subsequent session there will add to your store of knowledge about the

water. The more one fishes a water the more one gets to know its moods and the movements of the fish, and as time passes your catches should improve. Knowledge can also be gleaned from other anglers who may have fished the water for many years, but pick your time carefully when you pose your questions, for no angler wants to be distracted when he is expecting a bite at any second!

Knowledge of a water is not gained just by fishing. Spend time looking round the banks, and get to know the underwater contours. This is essential, for fish have regular patrol routes from one area to another.

Contours can best be studied from a boat, but alternatively you can use the bankside trees. A fair survey can be made by climbing into a tree for a good view; by wearing polarised sunglasses you will gain a lot of information on what is happening beneath the surface. The darker areas often indicate deeper water, but these places are not necessarily the best for catching fish, which invariably move into the shallows when feeding. Periods of drought should not be wasted, as at these times the water level may drop dramatically and you will be able to obtain a lot of useful information about the lakebed.

Lilypads and rushes protruding from the surface can produce giveaway signs of feeding fish. A shoal of rudd may be spotted as it splashes on the surface, and carp will be clearly seen as they cruise about, occasionally allowing a dorsal fin to appear above the surface. A carefully presented floating crust might well become a centre of interest for these fish.

On lakes, good swims can be found round the places where feeder streams enter the water. The movement aerates the water, small fish are attracted to the spot and roach and bream shoals occasionally move in. Pike and perch are also to be found here, feeding on the smaller fish.

There are times when fishing into the wind is effective, for the wind blows floating material into the bank. This surface drift causes the lower layer of water to move in compensation, and the movement along the bottom stirs the mud and with it various aquatic life, so fish can be expected to feed there.

Reading the banks can be as informative as reading the water. Popular swims can often be recognised by the well-trodden

Below: *The narrow point of an island is a popular lake fishing spot. The fish feed more readily because they are never far from the security of the deep water.*

margin where the grass has been trampled. Rushes may have been broken to create gaps through which to fish. This does not mean, however, that it is a good swim; it may be part of a regularly fished match venue. If you know matches are held there it is wise to avoid them on weekends, when most matches take place.

On lakes with extremely clear water sport can often be slow. One answer to this is night fishing, which may bring better results. Before actually going night fishing the lake should be visited in daylight so that you can become familiar with the place. Walk the bank, note the steep parts and the crumbly areas. Select the swim in daylight, too, and even practise a few casts to find the depth. On the night when you intend to fish, try to arrive before darkness to that the rods and tackle can be assembled and your fishing station settled. Before that, of course, make sure that night fishing is allowed on the lake!

Small, shallow lakes, mere ponds, are very often rich in natural food for fish. As well as the usual stillwater species, crucian carp thrive in these confined waters. Another fish found here is the rudd, and small ponds can easily become over-populated with small adult rudd. Eels and the occasional big perch may also live in these shallow ponds.

Above: *Small natural or well-established ponds, not too deep, suit the tench; the best swims are often among the lily beds.*

Reservoirs

Old-established reservoirs are like natural lakes. These waters can be flooded valleys or huge, man-made concrete bowls. All hold fish, and some harbour exceptional specimens.

Inlets and outlets are often marked by concrete structures, and below the waterline these are usually covered by weed harbouring snails and aquatic insects. These make perfect food for fish, which are never far away. At the same time the predators, pike and perch, will be nearby preying on the smaller fish.

The sloping banks of some reservoirs can be dangerously slippery, but they are worth fishing, for they hold all kinds of insect life upon which fish feed. The dam wall, where the water is deepest, is often out of bounds to anglers, so be sure to check any noticeboards.

Gravel pits

The demand for gravel and sand over the years has created a large number of huge, sometimes very deep holes in the form of worked-out pits. Many have been left to nature, which soon shows in the form of reeds, rushes, grasses and bordering shrubs, all of which take over and disguise the unsightly scars. Many gravel pits have been extremely well landscaped, almost right from the start of gravel extraction. Some pits have been planted with ten-year-old trees round the banks and the water has been stocked with quality fish such as roach, carp, pike and perch.

Because the gravel pit lakes are mainly on private land, or property owned by the gravel companies, most of the waters are rented out to angling associations. The members of these bodies are usually responsible for the maintenance of the banks and control of the fish stocks.

The depths of gravel pits vary considerably. Some are very deep, which means that rooted aquatic plants may be restricted to the edges. Some pits are generally shallow and have deepish channels, depending upon how the gravel was extracted. These pits make fine fisheries, with swims of varying depth to suit different species.

Alder bushes and willows that have become established round the banks afford shelter from wind and provide a screen to give anglers cover. This bankside vegetation is really valuable to anglers when the banks are low. Some fish feed close in to the bank and to catch them anglers must keep well back and use the vegetation as cover.

The quality of the water in pits is usually excellent and clear. When looking for a swim, look around in the vicinity of the weedbeds. If there are lilypads present, fishing close to their large floating leaves can be successful, for most fish are attracted by the cover from the plants and the food items they find among the vegetation.

Because depths vary so much it will pay to spend time walking the bank. Using the plummet in a systematic manner will enable you to draw a plan of the pit which will prove invaluable when you are choosing swims.

Early season fishing on a gravel pit is usually best for tench. Through the summer big carp will be the fish to go for, and as autumn approaches and winter begins the roach, perch and pike will be the main quarry.

Above: *Gravel digging has created many fishable still waters in areas where natural lakes are infrequent. Well established gravel pits, stocked with quality fish, are very popular with angling clubs.*

Most gravel pits hold tench. Some of the heaviest recorded specimens have come from these waters, which are ideally suited to the tench's life-style. Early morning and late evening are the best fishing times, when the tench come in close to the bank to feed. Many of the good tench swims in gravel pits are close to weedbeds.

Carp fishing methods can range from fishing the margins to long-distance casting. Where the reeds or rushes spread out in a thick mass from the bank in the shallows it indicates a useful swim for perch. These colourful predators feed on the small fry which congregate in the cover of the stems and leaves.

Most fish species are inactive during the winter, and the pike, perch and sometimes roach offer the best sport. If the temperature drops to freezing point, stillwater fish tend to stop feeding and the fishing can become very difficult.

Above: *The banks, holes and channels left in the pit bed by the gravel extraction machinery create a good range of swims.*

Below: *An old gravel pit develops like a natural lake, with dense patches of lilies and thick reedbeds that harbour a variety of fish.*

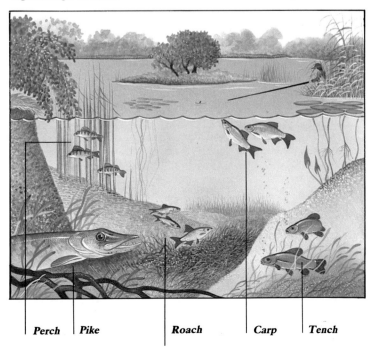

Perch | *Pike* | *Roach* | *Carp* | *Tench*

49

CONCEALMENT

Wherever they are, most fish are quick to detect danger and dash out to safe water, so all swims must be approached stealthily. When at the water, every attempt must be made to remain concealed from the fish, and no experienced angler will stand or sit with his body silhouetted against the sky. It is also good practise to do all the tackling up well away from the water.

Most anglers, except those dedicated stalwarts who prefer to fish on the coldest of winter days, consider it pleasant to sit and fish on a

Above: *On clear, shallow streams the angler should make the most of any cover offered by the vegetation.*

bright, sunny day. But as time passes the sun will change its position, and you should be aware that its movement can eventually throw your shadow on to the water, and even over the swim. Any movement that you make will then be very obvious to the fish, which may be frightened away.

Sometimes the danger of creating a shadow can be avoided if you dispense with the fishing stool or basket and sit

Below: *A centrepin reel does not release line as easily as a fixed-spool, so when casting the first stage is to pull a loop of line off the reel ①. Sweep the rod to the right so the end tackle swings back ②,*

then swing the rod forward and up so the tackle flies forward ③, releasing the loop at the same time so the line flows out through the rod rings ④. Drawing off two loops will give more length to the cast.

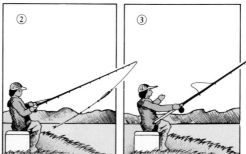

on the grass, thereby reducing the chance of throwing a shadow across the water. You can also move back, away from the water's edge.

If the sun moves round in front of you to shine in your eyes, polarised glasses will be worth their weight in gold. The glint and sparkle of rippling water can make concentration on the float very difficult and uncomfortable, but polarised glasses will filter out the stray rays and reduce eyestrain.

CASTING

The action the angler imparts with the rod to get the baited hook and terminal tackle out to the swim is called casting. There are a number of techniques, and which one to use will depend on the distance required and the equipment being used.

A good casting action should be smooth and precise; the line should be released at exactly the right moment for the tackle to go in the right direction. Accuracy is needed too, so that the hookbait falls into the water in the correct place, over the groundbait which has been thrown in previously. Obviously, the weight of the tackle helps in achieving distance, both in float fishing and legering. The action, distance and accuracy will also be helped if the outfit – rod, reel and line – is well matched.

Centrepin reel

When using a centrepin to cast float tackle, use your free hand to draw off a loop of line from between the bottom ring and the first intermediate ring, holding the line away from the rod. The baited tackle will then hang from the rod tip. To cast, swing the rod to one side, and the tackle will swing back like a pendulum. As the tackle starts to swing forward again, make the cast by bringing the rod round to the front with a sideways movement, keeping it well up.

As the tackle reaches the end of its forward swing its weight will exert a pull on the line; this is the time to release the loop, and the tackle's momentum will carry it out into the swim. As it reaches the water, lower the rod-tip, and the tackle will sink down to enter the water without creating too much disturbance. The float should then be held in check for a second or two to allow the bait to sink as naturally as possible.

If you are trotting the stream, pay the line off the reel to allow the tackle to run with the current. The strength of the stream is usually sufficient to pull line smoothly off a centrepin, and the speed can be controlled using a finger on the drum as a brake.

To achieve a longer distance with float tackle when casting with a centrepin, draw off two or even three loops of line from between the rod rings. As the final outward swing of the cast is made, release the loops consecutively starting with the top, or first loop. Timing is essential with this style, and practice is needed to get it right, but when it is mastered distances of two or three rod lengths can be regularly achieved.

Fixed-spool reel

The loop method is not to be recommended when using a fixed-spool reel because loose line is liable to tangle round the spool, spindle, handle or bale arm, ruining the cast

and creating birds' nests which are very difficult to unravel. In any case a far smoother, more efficient cast can be made directly from a fixed-spool. Use the same action as with the centrepin, but without drawing off the loops. Keep the bale arm open, and prevent the line spilling off until the final phase by clamping it against the spool or the rod with the forefinger. A single-handed action can be used, especially when casting a spinner, plug or leger rig.

Some anglers prefer the overhead cast, particularly when long-distance casting. To do this, swing the tackle behind you, with the rod pointing skywards, the bale arm open and a finger trapping the line. A strong forward swing of the rod will loop the line over and out, at which point it should be released to send the tackle out into the swim. This cast is best made with the fixed-spool reel.

Special techniques

When using a long pole, sometimes called a roach pole, with a fixed line and no reel, double-handed casting is required. The action can be either overhead or underarm.

For spinning, the fixed-spool or multiplier reel is used. Spinning rods are usually shorter than float or leger rods, and are ideal for single-handed casting. When using a tiny spinner the line needs to be extra-fine if any distance is needed. Generally, casting slightly upstream and across is the best way to present the lure to the fish.

LEGERING

This is a method of fishing a bait right on the bottom and can be practised in almost all kinds of waters. Legering is a good method for taking specimen fish as well as a big bag of medium bream, tench or barbel.

Because of their feeding habits, the chances of catching the bigger fish are greater when fishing on the bottom, so some form of weight is needed to hold a bait there. The most widely-used weight is the Arlesey bomb, but other weights are more effective in different waters and conditions. Whichever is chosen, the weight must be no heavier than is needed to hold bottom.

A leger weight should be free-running on the line so that when a fish picks up the bait it does not feel any resistance. The weight is stopped from running down on to the hook by a split-shot, or a swivel tied into the line above the hook.

In swims where the river is fast the flow will straighten the trace from the leger weight down, and the baited hook will waver about in the current downstream, but a little movement will not matter. In slower waters it pays to shorten the trace, because the

Below: When casting with a fixed-spool reel it is essential to keep the line under control. As the rod is swung back, use one finger to clamp the line against the rim of the spool; the bale arm should be open ①.

Stopping the backward sweep of the rod ② causes the tackle to swing back, bending the rod to provide power for the forward cast ③. As the tackle shoots forward, release the line ④.

line may not be pulled out and will lie in coils. If this happens, a fish can pick up the baited hook without a bite being registered above the surface.

After casting out, and taking up the slack line, lay the rod in rests with the tip near or under the water, and pointing downstream away from the bait. A bite will be indicated by a movement of the rod tip, by an indicator fitted on the rod, or by the line where it enters the water.

For most species, use an average leger rod with a fixed-spool reel holding at least 100 yards (90m) of 4lb (1.8kg) b.s. nylon; when casting heavy swimfeeders, the line strength should be increased to about 8lb (3.6kg) b.s. Legering is also an efficient way of fishing at long range on a large lake or reservoir, but since some 200 yards (180m) of line will be required a reel with a big capacity will be necessary.

Legering for small carp requires only general-purpose tackle and

Above: *A leger rod should be laid on rests at an angle, pointing away from the bait. In windy conditions the swingtip should be kept close to the water, or just submerged.*

simple leger rigs, but the equipment for big carp is rather more specialised. It is often a waiting game needing a lot of concentration, and it is a good plan to use a two-rod set-up: a pair of identical rods of 11-12ft (3.3-3.6m) in carbon or hollowglass, each with a 1¾lb (0.8kg) test curve, fitted with suitable fixed-spool reels loaded with 200 yards (180m) of 8lb (3.6kg) b.s. line. Electronic bite alarms are recommended.

Heavier, more powerful rods are needed when the water is exceptionally snaggy, or when you are fishing a bait directly into an area where there is a major hazard such as a submerged tree or a bed of lilies. In these circumstances strong pulling tactics will be needed to extract a big carp. Remember too that with a

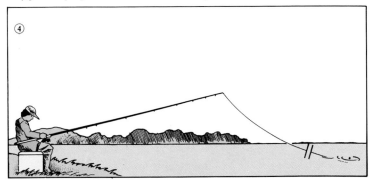

powerful rod you will have to have matching reel and line, for while the rod may be able to take the strain, the line will have to withstand the strength of the fish and cope with the underwater hazards of the swim.

Upstream legering

Sometimes, the only way of fishing a bait in an inaccessible swim is by the upstream leger style. This method is not exactly upstream, but up and across the river or stream, but it is always known as upstream legering for convenience.

A light leger weight should be used with this method, which is just heavy enough to hold bottom. The tackle is cast upstream of the angler's position, and the rod laid on the rests positioned so that it is pointing away from the bait, downstream and across the river.

With the rod in this position the effect on the take is that a fish picking up the bait will not feel as much resistance as it would if the bait were presented by standard downstream legering. This is because fish normally lie or swim facing upstream, except when turning to drop down to another part of the river. With upstream legering, therefore, as a fish takes the bait and drifts downstream towards

Below: *Upstream legering involves casting up and across the stream, using the lightest lead that will hold bottom. The bait trails back downstream, and a taking fish feels hardly any resistance.*

the rod top the effect on the line will be a slackening, and the fish will not feel any resistance as it would if the bait were being fished downstream. The bite will be more confident too.

At the moment that the line slackens, the angler must strike, with the rod horizontal and with a sweeping action downstream. This legering style is often very successful.

Rolling leger

The rolling leger technique enables a large swim to be searched without retrieving and recasting, which can disturb fish in a swim. It can be used in rivers where there is a fairly strong flow, employing a pear-shaped weight or a bomb. The tackle is cast to the top, upstream end of the swim, and the rod-tip is kept low to allow the bait to rest for a few minutes.

If no bites occur, raise the rod-tip to bring the line taut, and as the weight is slightly lifted the current will carry it along. Allow it to move a few feet, then lower the rod again to settle the weight back on the bottom. Wait for a further few minutes and then repeat the manoeuvre until you find the area where the fish are feeding. The weight should be heavy enough to just hold bottom against the flow. A swivel, as fitted to the Arlesey bomb, will help keep the line free from twist as the weight rolls about.

The rolling leger is thus worked down and through the swim. It is a fine means of searching through a weirpool with its circular eddies.

Above: *Rolling leger needs a light lead on a swivel, which will roll along the bottom in the current. In slower streams the weight is lifted so it drifts downstream.*

By varying the distance of each cast, a very large area can be covered.

When using the rolling leger in the strong waters of a weir it is sometimes necessary for the rod to be held high to keep as much line as possible clear of the water. This prevents the line from being carried round above the static leger, which can make striking difficult owing to too much slack line.

Often the current is strong enough to trundle the tackle down and across the stream without interference by the angler. When this happens the rod tip will keep 'nodding' – a movement which indicates the constant changing of tackle position. These movements should not be confused with real bites, which are usually sharper.

When making up your rig it is wise to incorporate a quick-release swivel into it. This will allow you to make a change of weight easily and quickly without having to dismantle the complete terminal tackle.

The use of groundbait is an important part of the legering technique, and it can be employed in a special way. It often pays to squeeze a portion of groundbait round the leger weight before the tackle is swung smoothly out to the swim. A combination of breadflake on the hook and bread groundbait on the leger weight, to crumble away near the baited hook, can account for some good quality fish, especially roach.

Swimfeeder technique

Another effective method of taking bottom-feeding fish is the swimfeeder leger technique. A stronger line is

Below: *A swimfeeder can be connected by a short length of nylon, or clipped directly to the main line by a swivel which may be held in place by locking shots.*

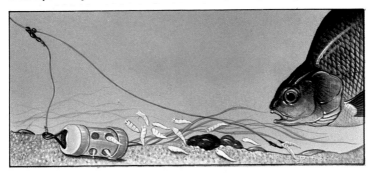

Above: *Using one rod rest and keeping one hand on the leger rod permits instant reaction to a bite.*

needed here for casting the heavy swimfeeder packed with bait.

In fast water the flow will soon empty the feeder and, assisted by the current, the bait items will trickle along the bottom, some finding their way to the area around the baited hook. The faster the current, the longer the trace or hook-link should be, to allow the loose bait particles to come to rest near the hook. A larger swimfeeder can also be used to increase the amount of maggots or feed released into the swim.

When the feed is to be all maggots, the blockend feeder will be the best pattern. It sometimes pays to enlarge the holes in the feeder, particularly in stillwater, and in this case casting should be more frequent to allow for the faster rate of feed discharge. Of course, with larger holes the maggots begin to wriggle out as soon as you have packed them in. This can be prevented to a certain extent by ducking the feeder in the water immediately before casting out.

When using a swimfeeder in conjunction with a swingtip a smaller, lightweight model may be preferable. This should, of course, be refilled and recast more frequently in order to maintain a good quantity of feed round the hook. Casting must be as accurate as possible in order to concentrate the feed. A widespread pattern of feed keeps the fish dispersed, which is exactly what you do not want.

Although the swimfeeder puts the groundbait where it will be most effective, it does not deposit enough feed to hold the fish in the swim. There will be times when it is necessary to place additional offerings of bait in the swim by using a catapult, or by throwing it in by hand. Whichever method you use, accuracy is vital if you are to attract fish to the swim and hold them there.

Swing-tipping

The sensitivity of bite indication when legering is improved when a swingtip rod extension is fitted. This extension, as well as the quivertip and springtip, will immediately register all bites from bottom-feeding fish.

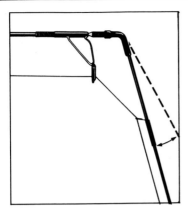

Above: *The swingtip is attached to the screw fitting in the tip ring by flexible rubber tubing.*

After the baited tackle has been cast out, and has settled on the bottom, turn the reel handle a few times to put tension on the line to the swingtip. If you find that the pull of the current is rather strong and the extension is being straightened, change to a stronger swingtip. If you do not have one, wrap a length of lead wire round the tip to help counteract the effect of the current. The weight should be adjusted so that the swingtip hangs just off the vertical.

The rod should not be pointed towards the bait, but placed on two rests positioned so that when the rod is resting on them the line goes out at an angle. When the line tension is adjusted correctly the swingtip or other extension will show the slightest movement created by a taking fish.

Bite indications will vary according to the strength of the bite. When fish are shy, their bites will hardly move the tip and the line may do no more than give a faint twitch. A fish that picks up a bait as it is moving towards the angler, as in upstream legering, causes the line to slacken with the result that the tip will fall back. No matter whether the tip straightens, the line slackens, or the tip barely twitches, a strike should be made. In fact, it pays to strike at any unusual movement of the tip.

FLOAT FISHING

Float fishing enables an angler to present a hooked bait at any depth from the surface to the bottom. It can be practised in every kind of water from fast streams to stillwater.

Trotting the stream

When fishing running water using float tackle the bait is cast upstream of the swim, allowed to drift down with the current, then retrieved and cast again – a technique known as trotting.

The float should be adjusted so that it holds the bait clear of the bottom, because it is more likely to be taken by the fish at midwater, although much depends upon the nature of the water – whether it is weedy, clear, or coloured with small suspended particles that impair the fishes' vision.

Below: *When trotting the stream keep a tight line on the float to ensure the bait precedes it through the swim. This permits a direct strike when a fish takes the bait.*

Find the depth of the swim using a plummet. Clip-on plummets are limited in practice to light tackle, and the traditional cone-shaped design is generally more efficient. Thread the hook through the eye and embed the barb firmly in the cork at the base. Swing the tackle out with an underarm action, then lower it to the bed of the swim – the line will go slack when it touches bottom. Retrieve the tackle and adjust the float for depth, then try again. Repeat the procedure until the float is positioned to fish the bait at the right depth.

By plumbing the depth yard by yard it is possible to build up a picture of the entire swim; ledges, holes and shallows can be found, and it may even be possible to 'feel' areas of gravel or sand.

Before starting to fish it often pays to introduce some groundbait or loose hookbait samples to get the fish interested and feeding, so that your baited hook will not suddenly appear where before there was nothing.

A smooth cast – so as to avoid throwing the bait off the hook – should place the tackle slightly upstream of the swim. The rod is kept pointing towards the float as it starts its journey; as it approaches, a lot of slack line will form, and this can be prevented by raising the rod as the float passes, then lowering it as it makes its way downstream. Do not allow the line between rod tip and float to go too slack as it passes, for if you get a bite at that moment it may well be impossible to strike because there is too much line to be taken up.

At every cast, toss a few maggots or casters in slightly above the top of the swim. The idea is to get the fish accustomed to seeing food particles there and so be induced to start feeding.

During its journey down, the float should be slightly retarded to ensure that the baited hook runs down before it, so that when a fish takes the strike can be made with the rod-tip directly

in line with float and hook. At the same time, holding the float back ensures that the sequence is right, for an unhindered float on the surface will travel downstream faster than a hooked bait close to the bottom, owing to the turbulence created down there.

At the end of the trot-down the float should be checked to allow the current to swirl the bait round attractively. Very often the bites occur as you do this, just before retrieving the tackle, because the fish have followed the bait downstream, catching up with it and taking it as it stops moving.

Right: *Long trotting a bait beneath overhanging trees and branches on the far bank is often an excellent method for catching chub.*

When the stream has a fast flow, maggots thrown in loose do not reach the bottom until they have been swept some distance downstream, and this is where the baitdropper can be used to get bait particles near the hookbait. The maggots from the baitdropper will trickle along the bottom, and when your hookbait is moving among them you have a good chance of hooking a fish.

Many rivers have long, streamy runs with bright, clear water. In these conditions the fish are wary, so it is advisable to keep well upstream of the area where the fish are.

Long trotting

This method is similar to trotting the stream, except that the float is allowed to run quite a long way downstream, working through bankside pools, under overhanging branches, or along the edge of a turbulent stream.

Plenty of line is needed on the reel, and a fairly big float must be used, first to control the passage of the baited hook as it runs downstream, and secondly so that it can be clearly seen at the far end of the run. To carry the amount of shot required to keep the bait down an Avon float is ideal, and as it is carried downstream it will pull line smoothly off the reel.

It is impossible to use the plummet to find the depth when long-trotting, so some means of trial and error must be employed to assess how deep the river is where your float will pass. This can be done by sending the baited hook down the swim and adjusting the float after each run down until it presents the bait just above the bottom. The riverbed is not likely to maintain an even depth through the run, and it is more important that the bait is at the correct depth at the end of the trot rather than at the beginning.

The baited hook must be allowed to travel freely and naturally along with the current, in company with hookbait samples that are thrown into the top of the swim at almost every cast. Bites are usually unmistakable; have no hesitation – make a quick, sweeping strike, then keep a tight line and bring the fish smoothly back to the bank.

Many experts prefer the centrepin reel for trotting, particularly long-trotting, for they claim that a smoother trot can be achieved with this kind of reel as the line rolls off the revolving drum. In addition, retrieving the terminal tackle can be speeded up by 'batting' the reel drum – using the palm of the hand to spin it from the rim. This keeps the drum turning rapidly and the float tackle is recovered smartly along the surface.

Below: *Float tackle can be worked well down the stream by long trotting. The float should be kept slightly in check so the bait moves ahead with the loose feed samples.*

Sliding float

If you want to fish a swim that is deeper than the length of the rod you will have to use a sliding float. It makes casting easier, and you will be able to fish at a greater distance.

The sliding float is usually an antenna type; the waggler is a popular pattern. Pass the line through the base ring, and use a short length of line of about the same breaking strain to form a sliding stop-knot. Trim the loose ends of the knot to about ¼in. (6mm), and adjust it on the line to retain the float in position, so that it fishes the bait at the correct depth. Make sure that the base ring is small enough to prevent the knot slipping through.

During the cast the slider float will drop down to the shot, which makes accurate casting easier. Once the tackle hits the water, keep the line slack so that the float lies flat on the surface. The terminal tackle and shots will drop down, pulling the line through the ring until the stop-knot reaches the float, and holds the bait where the fish are feeding.

If the float is weighted correctly it will ride on the surface with the tip just visible out of the water. When the float is in position and the bait is being fished, lower the rod top while slack line is taken up; then sink the line beneath the surface. Some degreasant

*Above: **Marginal reedbeds of lakes and rivers often harbour pike, perch or zander which will eagerly take a livebait on a float paternoster rig.***

can be used, or a little mud rubbed on the line will ensure that it sinks.

You can now place the rod on two rod rests or hold it. Watch the float keenly, because with so little of it showing above the surface, bites can be as quick as lightning. Holding the rod sometimes helps your concentration and enables a strike to be made immediately. If it is on the rests your hand should be poised above the handle, ready to lift and strike at the slightest twitch.

Float paternoster

This method is used to present a bunch of worms or a live fish bait for pike, perch or zander in a river or stream. Both rod pattern and main line breaking strain depend on the species sought. Obviously they will need to be stronger for pike than for perch. With the float paternoster a long rod is better than a short one.

Attach an Avon float to the line, then a three-way swivel. Use a line b.s. of about 4lb or 6lb (1.8-2.7kg) from the swivel to the paternoster weight. Some anglers prefer a much lighter line here because it will break

Above: *When fishing a livebait for zander on float paternoster tackle, use a float of the Avon type to keep the rig straight.*

enough the tackle can be simply lowered from the rod top straight down into the holes or gaps in weedbeds, by the side of lily pads, or close by an undercut bank. These places are difficult to fish by the usual float or leger fishing methods.

When fishing a livebait, a useful tactic is to feed the swim with loose maggots or a cloudbait. These will attract and hold a shoal of small fish, and their feeding movements will attract the larger predators. These will close in, the shoal will disperse and with luck your tethered livebait will be taken by the hungry predator.

Bite detection

When float fishing, some anglers expect the float to plunge beneath the surface before they strike. This is the traditional 'bite' as understood by non-anglers. But bites can vary considerably with the species being sought and the method of fishing employed at the time.

Sometimes the float does dip smartly, to disappear before the angler strikes. When the float tackle is being trotted down the stream, however, the float may merely hesitate or waver as if the tackle has brushed some weed – it could be a bite, but often it is not, and it is difficult to know when to strike. The float may be riding smoothly, then suddenly it will dip or flicker to one side, indicating a possible bite. River fish are used to intercepting items of food as they sweep downstream, and if they take the bait the float will make a definite unnatural movement.

The effect of a bite when float fishing in stillwater can be quite different, due to the feeding methods of fish in circumstances where their food items tend to drop down, rather than flow along with the stream.

The float might sink slowly until it disappears, or it may move slowly along the surface, or it can suddenly lift and lay flat. At times it will simply plunge out of sight. Each of these indications will require an appropriate reaction on the part of the angler, such as striking up if the float is dipping, or sideways away from a float being pulled along the surface.

first when a snag is caught, thus saving the main reel line. The middle arm of the swivel receives the hook link, which should be of main line b.s., and the hook is tied to the end.

The size of hook, whether single or treble, depends on the quarry expected. Almost any small fish can be used as the livebait, but it must be lively. Adjust the tackle so that the baitfish will be held swimming on the trace about 2½-3ft (75-90cm) clear of the river bottom.

This method is ideal when you are not static, but roving the bank and searching for pike or perch. The bait is cast underhand, or if the rod is long

BOAT FISHING

The best way of fishing a good swim situated in the main stream of a wide river is by boat. Although such swims can be reached by long-casting a leger rig, the natural presentation of float-fished tackle often brings more success. Presented this way the hookbait travels down with the current along with other matter, and the fish do not have to seek it, but take it in a natural manner as it approaches.

Many good roach swims are out of reach of the bank angler using float tackle. A boat enables him to get close to those swims and fish accurately and comfortably.

For fishing purposes, a boat should carry two anchors capable of holding the craft in a position across the stream in flowing water. The boat should be taken upstream and allowed to drift back down to the selected swim without creating disturbance with engine or oars. When the correct spot is reached – no closer than is necessary for accurate casting – the anchors are lowered gently into the water to hold it across the current. For the sake of quietness use nylon rope rather than chain for the anchors.

Boat anglers must make every attempt to remain as quiet as possible. The continuous shuffling of feet, the clatter of fishing accessories on the bottom of the boat, unnecessary splashing of keepnets, or indeed any unusual noises, even loud talking, can scare all the fish right away from the swim. Stealth is essential.

Long-trotting from a boat is pleasant, fairly easy and comfortable. A 10ft (3m) rod coupled with a centrepin reel is ideal. Make a start by going well upstream before fishing, then if the fish are elusive, raise the anchors just enough to allow the boat to drift quietly down with the current to the next swim. By this means, there will be no creaking of rowlocks, splashing of oars, throb of a noisy outboard motor, or any undue disturbance which may spoil the angler's chances. With the boat anchored across the stream where there is a good flow, the groundbait can be dropped over the side to trickle down the swim with the hookbait.

Boat fishing is also a fine and successful way to fish a large lake. Where there are islands present there will be many swims that bank anglers could never fish, either because of the distance or because of hazards which could ensnare the line or tackle.

SPINNING

Spinning is a mobile fishing style which can be employed at any time, particularly for pike, perch, zander, and occasionally chub. The lures used come in a tremendous variety of shapes, colours and sizes. Some lures wobble, while others just spin as they are drawn through the water, but they are all known as spinners.

Spinning rods are usually shorter than those used in float or leger fishing; a two-piece rod of 8ft (2.5m) is about average. Most casting reels can be used, but the most popular are the fixed-spool types. Line strength depends, as usual, on the species being sought, and should always be the lightest possible.

When making up tackle for spinning it is essential to incorporate at least one swivel, plus an anti-kink lead or a celluloid vane. The threat of line twist is very real, even with a non-spinning lure such as a plug.

There is little advantage in standing at the water's edge making one haphazard cast after another. All you

will do is create such a disturbance that any fish there will move off. Spinning is a roving affair, and the angler should move along the bank searching all the likely spots for hungry predators. The edges of weedbeds, undercuts, the piles that once supported old landing stages, weirs – these are the spinfisher's domain. Try the slack water, the mouths of drains, tributary streams and sluggish backwaters. Pike, for example, like to lie in reedbeds and lily patches, where they remain motionless waiting to launch out in a fierce lunge upon some unsuspecting victim. As your spinner wobbles past, creating just the kind of vibrations in the water that a small, hurrying fish would make, the pike's highly-developed sense organs detect the signals and it bursts out of hiding to locate the prey with its binocular vision, home in and take it.

Accuracy is needed when spinning in likely pike haunts. It is easy to cast too far and snag the treble or double hooks in tough lily stems or even overhanging branches. The speed of retrieve must also be accurate, for it will control the depth at which the lure will travel. Vary the rate to sample different depths.

Perch are susceptible to a moving bait and a day's pleasant spinning for them should bring good results. Perch

Above: *Firmly anchored in midstream, a boat provides a perfect platform for fishing the fast, turbulent water of a large weirpool.*

usually gather together and move about in shoals. Sometimes a shoal of small perch will carry one or two quite large fish on the outside of the group, so a spinner cast there might tempt one of these. They will be picking off tasty little perch themselves, for these aggressive, predatory fish are notorious cannibals.

Big chub feed on minnows and small fish of all species, and a well-spun lure could prove a deadly bait for these powerful members of the carp family. The streamy runs in weirpools, millpools and similar places should be explored with a spinner or small plug.

When spinning and searching a river it pays to work in a downstream direction. The lure should be cast across the stream, and as it strikes the water a yard or two of line can be pulled off, allowing the lure to sink through the water. As the current takes it away beneath the surface, work it back trying all the while to make it move erratically, like a fish swimming against the flow. The more movement, the more interesting it will prove to a predator, waiting in the shadows for its next meal.

TROLLING

The biggest pike are found in the deep water in the middle of large lakes, but it is difficult to catch them by normal spinning methods which can only be used effectively round the edges and along the fringes of weedbeds. However, huge areas of deep water can be covered by trolling a lure such as a spinner or plug from a boat.

Most trolling is done by two anglers in one boat. This provides a measure of safety, and if it is a rowing boat one angler can fish while the other rows. This allows the one fishing to make full use of his rod and reel to put life and movement into the lure. A single angler has to row while his rod is propped up at the stern, and the lure is merely trailed in a lifeless fashion.

The ideal tackle for trolling is a 10ft (3m) rod fitted with an appropriate centrepin reel. Moving the rod from parallel with the water to high in the air will induce the lure to alter course, while paying out more line will enable it to work deeper. Different lures have different actions, and if trolling is to bring really good results a number of designs may have to be tried.

STRIKING

When a fish takes the hooked bait, signalling the bite by the movement of the line or the float, the angler reacts by striking. This is the moment when he pulls the barb of the hook into the jaws of the fish. Whether float fishing or legering, the strike is much the same. In both cases timing is vital, and comes with practice. Only experience will teach the angler when to strike, and when not to strike.

If there is slack line between the rod tip and the float or leger, the strike will merely take up the slack line; the disturbance will probably lead to the fish dropping the bait and fleeing. It is essential to take up any slack line before settling down to wait for a bite.

Trap the line before striking by holding it against the rod butt with the forefinger, or by pressing a finger on the reel spool. This will ensure that the hook can do its work. If the line is not trapped, a strike will simply pull more line off the reel and the fish will not be properly hooked, if at all.

Above: *A small boat is useful for fishing deep water using float tackle, or when trolling a lure.*

The beginner usually strikes too viciously, often breaking the line at its weakest point. The strike must be made in a controlled manner, firmly but gently. If the line still breaks the spool may have to be changed for one holding line of a greater breaking strain.

Once a fish has been successfully hooked the rod must be kept held up with the tip in the air. This allows the spring in the rod to absorb the struggles of the fish. Never allow the line to become slack, for if the barb is not set home properly the hook may slip free and you will lose the fish. Always be prepared for the fish to find some extra strength for a final burst of activity, especially when it sees the bank. Draw it steadily towards the submerged landing net.

LANDING THE FISH

Although landing the fish is a fairly straightforward operation some skill is required. It is not just a matter of dipping the net into the water to scoop the fish into the air. Such hasty netting is always risky, especially with large fish; they react violently as they feel the rim of the net and may break free.

Landing nets are available in all sizes, and it is wise to buy one as large as you can afford, and of soft, knotless mesh. There are nets on the market that can accommodate the largest pike

and carp. These need to be used with two hands – the rod can be put down once the fish is truly played out.

The wise angler assembles his landing net as soon as he is ready to commence fishing, and certainly does not wait until he has hooked a fish. It may be a big net, but it will be no use if it is not ready in time.

As you draw the fish in, sink the rim of the net quietly into the water before the fish is really close. When played out, a fish usually rolls on to its side; this is the time to draw it quietly over the sunken net. Once the fish is safely in, the net should be drawn well up so that the fish is right down and safe. Then take the net away from the waterside to remove the fish, carefully unhooking it.

Above: *When netting a fish draw it quietly over the submerged net rim before raising the net to secure it.*

Most coarse fish are returned alive to the water. They must always be handled with consideration, especially when disgorgers are used to extract hooks, and they should be put back as soon as possible. Take care when weighing a sizeable specimen to support it in a cradle of mesh, and always wet your hands before handling any fish, or you will damage it. A fish put back in such a state is vulnerable to disease, and may not survive for long. When putting it back hold it upright with its head upstream, or facing away from the bank, and support it until it swims away.

CHUB *Leuciscus cephalus*

Waters: Mainly rivers and weirpools, weedy channels, undercut banks; occasionally canals and, more rarely, lakes.

Baits: Bread, cheese, sweetcorn, hempseed, luncheonmeat, maggots, casters, minnows, crayfish, plugs, spinners.

Techniques: Float, leger, feeder-leger, free-lining, spinning.

This is a potentially big fish and although specimens of over 10lb (4.5kg) are extremely rare a surprising number of chub in the 5-6lb (2.2-2.7kg) class are caught each season, especially in rivers rich in their food-supply and with a strong current to enable powerful muscle to be built up.

A chub of this weight is a worthy opponent for any angler for it does not fall easily into taking a bait, but when it does it fights extremely hard. The fish will head for any weedbeds in the area, and if it is allowed to reach this security it will take skill and strong tackle to get it out into open water, where it can be brought to the net.

The big, blunt head and thick lips of the chub make it fairly easy to recognise. It has a strong, well-proportioned body with large, clearly marked scales. It is usually greenish-brown along the back, shading down to silvery flanks, at times rather brassy, and a silvery-white belly.

Small chub may well be confused with large dace, and many a small chub has been weighed in as a specimen dace. The practised eye, however, is aware that the dorsal fin is a sure means of specific identification. The chub's dorsal is convex, or outwardly rounded, while that of the dace is concave. The same applies to the anal fins of both species.

Chub are omnivorous. The immature fish will take insects and crustaceans, while the large, adult chub will feed on fish, large invertebrates such as crayfish, and even frogs and newts. In summer, when there is a rise of large flies, chub will take them from the surface in the manner of trout.

The usual livebait for chub is a minnow. This small fish can be lip-hooked or the barb may be passed through the back, or root of the dorsal fin. This bait can be trotted down with the current, or legered in the likely swims. But small livebaits are ideal for long casting. When using the minnow as a deadbait, it is lip-hooked or mounted on the hook by means of a baiting needle.

Above: *Legering for chub in a deep, steady-flowing river. The long rod is held at an angle to keep most of the line clear of the current.*

Below: *Coral red anal and pelvic fins against a silvery-white belly help to distinguish the chub – a fine fighting fish.*

Wasp grubs make highly attractive baits for chub of all sizes. The grubs can be float-fished singly, in twos, or – when seeking the really big, lone fish – as a bunch on a size 10 hook.

On some waters a crayfish is a particularly deadly bait for chub. It is most effective fished on leger tackle. When using live crayfish keep the

Above: *This average sized chub was taken on a float-fished bait of breadflake, trotted with the flow of the river.*

Right: *A medium flow river, not too deep, with overhanging trees on the far bank – an ideal spot for float fishing for chub.*

distance beteen the legerweight and the hook fairly short, the reason being that if its movements are not restricted the crayfish will crawl about and hide under stones or in the roots of weeds, thus putting your bait out of sight of any hungry chub. One useful tip about using crayfish as bait: when the creature is a medium-sized one a chub usually gives plenty of warning by nudging and mouthing the bait before finally taking it.

The angler needs to move quietly and fish without creating any undue disturbance because the chub is a shy fish. Approach the water cautiously, for some large chub may be hanging just below the surface and if they see your shadow they will disappear fast!

Overhanging willows make a likely chub haunt, so look out for one on the far bank within casting distance. Use float tackle and cast upstream as far as is practicable, then work the bait down to the area where the chub are lurking. Let the bait approach the area naturally – never cast directly into the swim, it will surely scare them off.

Weirpools are other likely spots. Here, the leger will find chub in the weir stream and at the eddying tail of the flow. Use the lightest leger weight that will hold bottom, cast upstream

and again work the bait down to the fish. A feeder-leger can be employed here, its contents acting to attract hungry chub to the hookbait.

Legering is a good method of fishing other river swims without the angler disclosing his presence to the fish. The free-running leger is often preferred, and because the chub has a large mouth a substantial bait is recommended – which, of course, also means a large hook. A size 8 or 6 is usually about right, and it is best if it is tied direct to the reel line.

If the swim is suitable, use a trace about 3ft (1m) long and select the lightest leger weight that will hold bottom in the current. All chub fishing must be done so that the bait is presented as naturally as possible.

No one can be sure how a chub will take a bait; it might just twitch the rod tip, or on the other hand it may give the rod a sudden, mighty thump. If the water is fast and streamy this last kind of bite is likely because a chub has to take an item of food quickly as it passes on its way downstream. In swims with a slow, or steady flow a quivertip may be used, but the bite might still turn out to be fierce and unexpected. Experience will indicate the strength of quivertip to use.

Some streamy runs and channels between weedbeds are best fished by float, and trotting the stream is often most effective. The chub almost always lie in the current, heads facing upstream, in midwater to intercept any item of food which is carried towards them.

When trotting the stream the bait can be cheese, sweetcorn, breadflake, casters – almost anything edible. Whatever the hookbait, a few samples should be fed into the swim at regular, frequent intervals. The bait size will depend very much on the size of chub expected, bearing in mind that they can take a very large bait in their capacious mouths. Such is the range of possible bait sizes that hooks will be from size 8 to 18. A rule of thumb is that when trotting the stream the bait need not be so large as when legering.

It is good technique to vary the depth at which you are fishing now and again, and hold the float back for a second or two as it is being trotted down the swim. This allows the bait to waver about in the current, a tactic that often induces a chub to take.

Another method of chub fishing is free-lining in a streamy run, allowing the bait to be swirled round and carried downstream into eddies and under overhangs of trees and banks. Extra weight can be added to leger the bait, allowing it to be trundled along the bottom. This style works well in weir streams.

BARBEL *Barbus barbus*

Waters: Rivers, weirpools, fast runs, clear channels between weedbeds, holes in undercut banks.

Baits: Bread, cheese, worms, casters, wheat, sweetcorn, hempseed, sausagemeat, luncheonmeat, crayfish, and small fish such as gudgeon and loach.

Techniques: Leger, float, float-leger, swimfeeder leger, rolling leger, tight corking.

The barbel takes its name from the two pairs of barbels on its upper lip, one pair at the corners of the jaws, the other towards the front. It is a powerful fish with a flattened belly, and well adapted to lying on the gravelly bed of a strong and fast-flowing river. The coloration is normally greenish-brown or bronze on the back, shading to a golden yellow on the sides, down to a yellowish-white belly.

The bottom-feeding habits of the barbel are indicated by its underslung mouth, the top jaw projecting well forward of the lower. The single dorsal fin is characterised by the leading spine having a heavy, strongly serrated edge; the tailfin is unevenly lobed. The lower fins are tinged with orange, with the rays of the anal fin noticeably long. There are small, well embedded scales and the eye is golden.

Barbel are large and powerful fish of the cyprinid family, able to reach weights of at least 15lb (6.8kg), but the average is about 5lb (2.3kg). Their tenacity and fighting ability are remarkable, and when the angler has hooked his first big barbel he may well think he has lodged his hook in a submerged tree, so doggedly do they resist capture.

Sport with barbel is rarely fast and furious, because more time is spent seeking them out than, for example, roach or dace. However, that time is well spent, and when a large barbel is finally hooked it will provide ample compensation by fighting its way right to the landing net.

Any hour from dawn to dusk is barbel time, but keen anglers prepared to fish after dark may have more success, for the fish tend to take a bait more boldly at night.

The barbel feeds by moving about the riverbed in search of snails, mussels, caddis and other insects,

Right: *The barbel is well adapted to bottom feeding – the underslung mouth and barbels suit its habit of searching the bottom for food.*

Below: *The barbel is a popular sporting fish widely distributed in Europe. It is often found in small schools of equal-sized fish.*

tadpoles, crustaceans and any small fish that can be caught on the bottom. For this reason they are usually caught with bottom-fished baits.

The leger is the best method of getting the bait down to where the fish are. A light weight that will just hold bottom should be used, the best kind being an Arlesey bomb or a pear-shaped weight attached to a swivel, particularly when you are working your hookbait through a swim. In fast water a flat leger weight will hold the bottom better.

Most of the quick-water runs that barbel prefer are too fast and generally too deep for float-fishing methods to be successful. Occasionally a swim can be found that suits the float tackle, and trotting tactics are usually the best

to use. A buoyant-enough float to carry a fair weight should be used to fish such a swim, to present a moving bait just off the bottom.

Whatever the technique used, a 10-11ft (3-3.3m) rod with an all-through action is vital, and it must be strong and pliable enough to absorb the shock of a plunging, fighting fish. It must also have power in order to apply pressure on a barbel straining to reach the security of a dense weedbed, tree roots or some underwater hideout.

The reel can be a centrepin or a fixed-spool, depending on personal preference, but the choice may be influenced by the nature of the swim and the fishing style. For instance, long-range legering is best done with a fixed-spool reel loaded with about 100 yards (91m) of 4-5lb (1.8-2.3kg) b.s. line for clear swims or 6-8lb (2.7-3.6kg) in snaggy water.

A round-bend hook with medium-length shank, eyed rather than spade end, is ideal, but it must be strong enough to hold a hard-fighting fish.

A well-proven barbel technique is to leger with a swimfeeder, packed with maggots which are washed from the feeder to trickle out and move through the swim on the current. Barbel move steadily into the swim, attracted by the loose offerings, and eventually find the baited hook. They have been occasionally known to mouth the feeder itself.

Bite indicators are not usually necessary, for the angler is given plenty of warning when a barbel bites – the rod top bends suddenly and very violently!

An old style known as tight-corking, or tight-lining, is ideal for barbel fishing in certain waters which have eddies and holes under the bank.

It can also be used in swims with a fair current and shallows some distance downstream from the angler.

A large Avon, or cork-bodied long-trotting float is very suitable since a leger weight and a few large split-shot are needed to keep the bait down when the float is held back. To fish this rig the depth must be plumbed, and the float adjusted so that the distance between float and weight is sufficient for 18-20in. (45-50cm) of line to lie on the bottom when the tackle is in the deepest part of the swim.

A few balls of groundbait laced with hookbait samples should be thrown in before starting to fish; a baitdropper could be used to do this. A couple of large redworms on the hook will usually bring results.

Cast out and work the tackle down to the swim, keeping the rod top up and the line tight, with the float in check. Use the current to keep the bait moving ahead of the float and rolling along the bottom.

As the tackle reaches the swim, hold it for a while, then allow it to run down yard by yard, pausing for a minute after each short run.

Once a barbel swim has been found, make a careful note of it. Certain swims in barbel rivers always hold a number of fish during the summer. In winter, barbel go into semi-hibernation, seeking deep, quiet water when it is very cold. After a spell of mild weather, and sometimes after a flood, they may well emerge and feed, and fish of 10lb (4.5kg) and over have been caught as late as December.

Below: *This catch of barbel was taken from a river of reasonable depth and flow. The catch was made at night using a legering technique.*

BREAM *Abramis brama*

Waters: Sluggish rivers, reservoirs, lakes, ponds, pits, canals.
Baits: Worms, maggots, bread, sweetcorn.
Techniques: leger, feeder-leger, float.

The common bream, also known as the bronze bream, is a fairly weighty fish, with specimens reaching over 12lb (5.4kg), but a good average is 5-6lb (2.2-2.7kg). It has a very deep and strongly hump-backed body, a long anal fin, a short dorsal and a deeply forked tailfin. The lobes of the tailfin are assymetrical, the lower one more rounded than the upper.

In colour, the bream is dark on the back, shading to a pale greenish-brown on the sides. The body is covered by a thick layer of mucus. Compared with the rest of the body, the eye is small.

The fish congregate in huge shoals which signal their presence by rooting around in the mud for food items, stirring up the water in muddy swirls. At other times the shoal will be seen as the fish roll and sport on the surface. When the experienced angler sees this behaviour, he knows he has time to tackle up, ready for when the bream go back down to feed.

In rivers, legering and float-fishing are equally effective, but several factors – speed of the current, whether the fish are feeding on or off the bottom, whether they will accept a stationary or moving bait – determine which method is likely to prove best.

Below: *A high, humped back, a generally oval-shaped body with flattened sides, and a comparatively small head make the common bream an easily recognizable fish.*

Where legering is decided upon there are two successful baiting methods. One way is to fish maggots or casters in conjunction with a blockend feeder packed with hookbait samples; the other is to pack the feeder with cereal groundbait and use a variety of hookbaits.

The blockend feeder (the Drennan Feederlink is recommended) is either fixed to the main line or allowed to slide along it. The distance at which the feeder is stopped from the hook is often critical, but a hooklink of 18-24in. (45-60cm) is adequate.

After packing the feeder with maggots, casters or hemp, cast it into the selected spot. It should be weighted just enough to hold bottom. A size 16 hook is used, attached to a 2lb (0.9kg) b.s. hooklink. If bites prove finicky reduce the length of the tail and tie on a smaller hook.

Always keep a keen eye open for bites as the hookbait is dropping through the water, and also immediately it touches bottom. Bites will not always occur at these times, far from it, but be prepared. If you know bream are in the swim and bites are just not coming, keep experimenting. Often it is the bait presentation that is at fault.

Bites will vary from small pulls to heaves that bend the rod-top right over. If a quivertip is being used, the thickness should be such that when the feeder is on the bottom the quivertip is only slightly bent.

Obviously you will get the same effect when using a carbon-fibre rod with a very fine tip. Do not delay the strike if the tip just moves a little, providing that it moves *slowly*. Small, insignificant bites often come from large bream.

Worms, breadcrust and flake can be presented on a size 12, 10 or 8 hook (the size, of course, depending on the bait), attached to 4-6lb (1.8-2.7kg) b.s. line. Groundbait can be breadcrumbs, hemp or both, introduced either in a swimfeeder or by a catapult.

One factor often overlooked is that bream feed in very confined areas, often no more than 4ft (1.2m) square. Although the bream may be rolling over an area of, say, 15yd (14m) their feeding area is very confined and success can only be assured if the bait is cast accurately into the same place every time. Where bream are concerned the ability to cast accurately is very important.

Another point to remember is the sequence when baiting up. Always place the maggots on the hook first, then fill the feeder. Filling the feeder first will result in many of the maggots falling out through the holes while the hook is being baited.

In recent years so-called 'high protein' baits have been extremely popular. Those with molasses and maple syrup flavourings are reckoned the most successful with bream. The flavourings are mixed either into bread paste or with maggots, and will often encourage bream to pick up a

Below: *A fine pair of bream taken from a large natural lake, proudly displayed for the camera.*

Above: *Silver bream (Blicca bjoerkna) is the smaller of the two bream species, and looks very similar to a young common bream. It is, however, seldom caught.*

bait which they would otherwise ignore. The choice of flavourings is vast and increasing all the time, but they will not, despite their reputation, guarantee success.

When float fishing, a waggler with a shot-loading of about two swan shot (SSG) should be enough. The shotting is important because no more than 1in. (25mm) of the float should show above the surface. Maggots and casters are presented on a size 16 or 18 hook, attached to 1½lb (0.7kg) b.s. line, or bread and worms are used on a size 12 or 14 hook, attached to 3lb (1.4kg) b.s. line.

The float is set so that the bait either trips along the bottom or travels just above it, the length of 'tail' about 20in. (50cm). Bites are usually decisive and the float either dives straight under or disappears slowly. Sometimes, if the fish lifts the bait, the float will rise a little out of the water.

If bites do not materialise, move the float down the line a little, so that the bait is riding higher in the water, or up the line so that the bait is fished lower. This will slow the bait down in a swim with flowing current. Vary the length of tail, or reduce the size of bait and, possibly, the hook size.

CARP *Cyprinus carpio*

Waters: Mainly lakes, gravel pits, ponds and reservoirs. Also deep, slow rivers and canals.

Baits: Bread (paste, crust, flake), potato, honeyed paste, worms, particle baits (sweetcorn, beans, peanuts, etc), luncheon meat, other high-protein baits.

Techniques: Legering, free-lining, floating crust.

Highly rated by anglers for its fighting qualities, the carp is a powerful thickset fish with a broad tail, and a toothed spine at the front of the dorsal fin. It has a long barbel at each corner of the mouth, and two smaller ones on the top lip. The colour is very variable, but usually brown-green on the back, shading to golden yellow on the flanks and belly.

Most carp are derived from a strain known as king carp, which were originally bred for the table. These fish put on weight quickly, and are known to reach over 60lb (27kg). There are three varieties: the common carp, which is a fully-scaled fish, the mirror carp, which takes its name from the few very big scales on its flanks, and the leather carp, which is almost scaleless. In rivers, the common carp does not reach the bulk of the stillwater varieties, being a sleeker fish, but it is still an extremely powerful fighter.

Carp fishing is one of the most advanced branches of today's big-fish scene. There are more carp about than ever before and the angler can fish for them in a variety of waters with every hope of catching big specimens, even fish over 20lb (9kg).

Although common carp occur in rivers and canals, it is lakes and gravel pits which provide the bulk of the sport. Some of them contain mostly small carp with a few over 10lb (4.5kg), while others hold fish of up to 40lb (18kg).

Generally, waters with mainly smaller carp tend to provide the most consistent sport, simply because there

Below: *The scale distribution of the mirror carp is highly variable, but is usually restricted to the top of the back and flanks.*

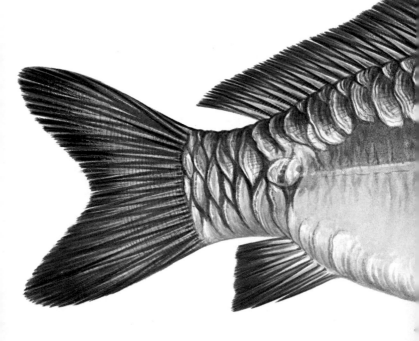

are more to catch. Big-carp lakes are a far more difficult proposition, with fewer fish caught in return for many hours of effort.

Anyone prepared to walk the bank quietly and stand watching the water in likely places can, over several seasons, accumulate useful information on the movements and feeding habits of the carp. After some time he will know the swims most likely to hold carp at any given period.

They are secretive fish with a liking for cover. Their favoured haunts include weedbeds and jungles of sedge and lilypads. Sections of bank overhung by low trees always attract carp, and so do islands. In a thickly weeded lake carp can be spotted as they move along the clearings between weed clumps. On a windy day the area of bank receiving the wind is often a feeding hotspot.

Gravel pits have great variations in depth, and without a knowledge of the bottom contours it can be very difficult to select a carp-holding area with confidence – especially in winter when surface activity is at a minimum.

Above: *This fine 21 lb (9.5 kg) mirror carp took a legered bait, fished in an artificial lake during the winter season.*

Depths from 4ft to 10ft (1.2-3m) are favoured by carp, rather than holes of maximum depth, so it follows that gravel bars are always 'carpy'. A bait

cast to lie on top of a bar or at one end is ideally placed to waylay a carp nosing along or over the bar.

Carp can be caught at any time of the day or night, but feeding spells tend to vary from water to water according to weather and water conditions. The most productive periods during summer are from late evening into full darkness, and from just before dawn into the morning. Morning sessions are often very rewarding because the carp are feeding in earnest; in winter, the feeding spells tend to occur during the mid-day period.

The simplest rig for carp is an eyed hook tied direct to the main line. This free-line set-up is used to present floating baits such as breadcrust, air-injected lobworms and so on, to attract surface feeders, or to fish a sinking bait such as a par-boiled potato at short range. A floating weight such as a wooden 'controller' is required for accurate long casting of floating baits.

For presenting baits on or near the bottom, the best general-purpose rig is a running link-leger. An Arlesey bomb is connected to a link-leger bead by 6in. (15cm) of nylon. The main line is run through this bead and then through a tiny plain bead before attaching a swivel. The 12-18in. (30-45cm) hook length, of similar b.s. to the main line, is tied to the free eye of the swivel. The rig is completed with a size 6 or 8 eyed hook.

In heavily fished waters, carp are not always confident feeders. Having been hooked before, they are often

Above: *This well-conditioned carp was taken on float-fished bait in a fairly large, slow river.*

wary and able to sense the difference between a free item and a bait attached to a hook in the normal way. An excellent method here is the hair rig, one of the most significant developments in carp fishing.

To fish a bait hair-rig style, the hook length is set at 12-18in. (30-45cm) and the bait is linked to the hook by 1½-2in. (4-5cm) of 1lb (0.45kg) b.s. nylon tied to the bend. When a carp is gently sucking up baits from the bottom, a bait on a hair will 'lift' in exactly the same way as the free offerings and may be taken well back into the fish's mouth. Should the carp then sense the danger, perhaps feeling the line on its lips, and blow the bait out, there is still a good chance of the hook pricking the fish's lips and sending it off on a fast self-hooking run. Hard baits are best for hair rig fishing.

Below: *With the hair rig, the wary carp sucks up the bait, which is linked to the hook by a short length of fine nylon.*

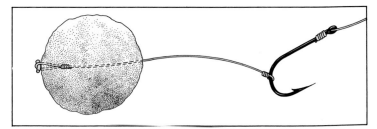

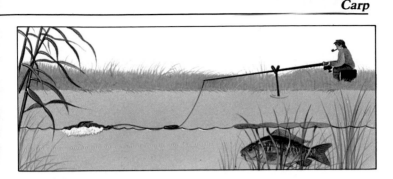

Above: *On summer days, carp cruise beneath the surface and suck down floating food items. They will often take a floating crust.*

Each rod is mounted on a pair of rests and the lines connected to one of the bite indicator arrangements. The bale arm of the reel is usually left open. Essential equipment includes a large landing net, and dial scales for accurate weighing of notable specimens.

Carp should be returned immediately to the water and held upright until they are able to swim off. When a carp is to be retained for any length of time, always use a keepsack

Below: *Dedicated carp anglers will spend several days – and nights – in this type of brolly tent, waiting for the big fish.*

of industrial nylon, 5×4ft (1.5×1.2m) punched all over with ¼in. (6mm) holes to provide adequate water flow. One fish per sack is the rule, and the sack should be pegged out in water not less than 3ft (1m) deep on a hard bottom. In hot weather retention time must not exceed one hour.

Carp enthusiasts often fish for a week or more at a time. Equipment for extended sessions should include a bedchair, a brolly tent, warm clothing, cooking gear and plenty of food and hot drinks.

Having tackled up, cast out and adjusted the indicators, carp fishing is a waiting game until one of the indicators signals a bite – anything from a brief twitch to a full-blooded, searing run. No two carp fights are the same, but when a hooked fish happens to be a big one the battle will be a memorable one.

TENCH *Tinca tinca*

Waters: Reservoirs, lakes, ponds, gravel pits, canals, sluggish rivers.
Baits: Maggots, worms, bread, sweetcorn.
Techniques: Float fishing, laying-on, float-leger, feeder-leger.

The tench is a thickset fish with rounded, spoon-shaped fins. Its colour varies from water to water. In most stillwaters, and particularly muddy lakes, tench are dark green; in clear gravel pits and lakes they are a bright greenish yellow. The body is protected by small, deeply-set scales and a thick layer of mucus. The mouth has two small barbels at the corners. It is a powerful fish, and has maintained its popularity with anglers because of its hard-fighting qualities as well as its handsome appearance.

Tench prefer weedy waters, especially those with dense patches of lilypads. Hook a large tench near one of these and the fish will dash straight for the security of the thick stems and leaves of the lilies, from which it will be difficult, sometimes impossible, to dislodge.

Most well-established lakes have a thick growth of weed in the shallows, which supports an abundance of natural food. On these waters, weed clearance and raking can help towards consistently good results. If carried out a few hours before fishing, tench will quickly return to the treated swim, and their presence will be indicated by groups of small bubbles, released as the fish probe into the disturbed mud for edible items. To hold the tench in such a swim, throw in small quantities of groundbait laced with hookbait samples. This will help to sustain the tench in a feeding mood – but take care not to overfeed them.

Gravel pits consistently produce much larger tench than the more traditional waters. Fish of 5-6lb (2.3-2.7kg) are now regularly taken, whereas a 4lb (1.8kg) fish would have caused some excitement 30 or 40 years ago. The stocking of tench into gravel pits has been carefully controlled over the past 25 years, reducing competition for natural food so that the naturally large stock fish put on weight very quickly.

This is fine, but with fewer fish, more knowledge of the water is required before real success in catching the big tench can be achieved. Polarised glasses are helpful when studying such a water. Find the

deep and shallow areas, and the channels running between or running alongside shallow banks. Try to compile a map showing the contours of the lake, or the areas to be fished. Indicate places of heavy weed growth, and areas of darker, deeper water. The map should suggest two or three likely places that can be reached easily.

Above: *This canal section, fairly shallow, clean water with a slight flow, holds several species of fish, including many fine tench.*

Below: *A strong, fighting fish, the tench has tightly packed, embedded scales covered with a layer of mucus. The fins have rounded edges.*

Above: *In stillwater laying-on is a good technique. Lighter baits can be fished higher in the water by moving the float down the line.*

The best time to fish for lake tench is during the dawn and dusk periods, but gravel pit tench seldom limit their feeding to these times – even the middle of a hot day will find a tench ready to accept a bait.

Where long and accurate casting is called for to reach the swim, legering techniques – with or without a swimfeeder – are essential. However, provided there is a reasonable depth of water within range, laying-on with float tackle is by far the most productive style for offering the larger baits such as bread, lobworms and sweetcorn. The float is moved up the line so that the bulk shot, and the bait, lies on the lake bed. Reeling in a little will tighten the line between the shot and the float, enabling bites to be detected easily.

The lighter maggots and particle baits should be suspended from the float just on or off the bottom, using slightly finer hook-lengths.

Tench are notorious for producing strange movements of the float. Large baits fished on the bottom being 'worried' by tench produce all kinds of movements ranging from small dips to runs of a yard or so. The fish may even lift the bait so that the float lies flat on the surface. But the patient angler waits until a positive bite occurs.

A firm strike must be made, and the instant the tench feels the hook it will make stubbornly for the security of the weeds, trying to bore deep into the roots. If it gets there you may be in trouble, and it must be stopped so that it can be played in clear water, where you have a chance. Prompt, skilful action should result in your landing a grand, sporting fish.

Left: *This trio of tench was taken using float fishing technique during an early morning session on a quiet stretch of canal.*

Above: *This angler is preparing to net a tench taken on a legered bait from a large lake of varying depth – an ideal tench water.*

ROACH *Rutilus rutilus*

Waters: Medium to slow-flowing rivers, lakes and reservoirs, canals and streams.
Baits: Bread, cheese, maggots, casters, hempseed, tares, wheat, sweetcorn, elderberry.
Techniques: Float (trotting, laying-on), leger, feeder-leger.

The roach is probably the most important coarse fish sought by anglers. It does not grow large – one of 3lb (1.3kg) is rare, although it can reach over 4lb (1.8kg) – and although the roach has a very wide distribution the bigger specimens are not at all common. One of 2lb (0.9kg) is regarded as the fish of a lifetime by most coarse anglers. The fish has a dark greenish back, with the flanks usually silvery, and the larger specimens have a brassy sheen. The fins are pinkish or orange, and the iris of the eye is red.

Roach-bream hybrids are very common in waters that hold both species, and when large hybrids have been caught they have often been claimed as roach rod-caught records only to be disallowed when proper identification has been made.

The hybrid is silvery, with even a bluish tint. It has a forked tailfin, typically a bream feature, as is the anal fin. The numbers of rays in the dorsal and anal fins are reliable clues to identity, but for absolute identification the pharyngeal bones must be removed and studied. This unfortunately means killing the fish, a process very reluctantly adopted if the fish is large.

Roach are shoal fish, so the angling technique is to get the shoal in the swim and hold it there by groundbaiting and feeding. The fish is a fast-biter, so expertise in striking is an asset to the angler.

Hempseed is a fine bait for roach, but although it brings the bites, they are often so quick that only a small percentage of the fish are hooked. So more usually the hemp is used as feed, or groundbait, while the hook is baited with a tare, a caster or an elderberry. Sometimes the roach will

feed near the bottom, close in under the rod top. This is the time to bring in the baitdropper, which can be used to good effect to keep a shoal of fish feeding in the swim.

Stewed wheat is often used in the autumn, especially for the bigger roach. Many anglers prefer maggots, using a technique of heavily feeding with lots of loose maggots The small roach in the swim gorge themselves on this feed and eventually move off. At this point, the big specimen roach move in, to be tempted by hookbait.

When trotting a float-suspended bait for river roach, use a fairly soft-actioned carbon rod with a centrepin reel. This tackle will enable you to obtain the best possible bait presentation, a point which is vital in roach fishing. The bait can be made to travel at the speed of the current, or it can be made to move very slowly across the bottom, to be coaxed over snags, ridges and weeds. This style is really deadly for big roach. The centrepin must have a large diameter to help line recovery, and if it is wide-drummed and without handles it will help to prevent tangles. Fewer tangles caused by wind action will be met if the line comes off the top of the drum rather than the bottom, and this will also give better line control.

The use of a centrepin restricts you to fishing close in, because the reel is not designed for casting to any distance. So when casting and trotting farther out the centrepin will have to be exchanged for a standard fixed-spool or a close-faced reel.

Terminal tackle is generally dictated by conditions on the day, but if you carry a good range of stick floats you will be equipped to fish most swims. The shot are normally spaced out evenly along the line between the float and a small hook.

For long-range roach fishing in both running and stillwater, use a

Below: *Favouring lowland lakes and rivers, but able to thrive in a variety of habitats, the roach is widely distributed. A slight hump develops on its back as it grows.*

straight waggler float with a fine peacock quill insert for sensitivity. In water down to 8ft (2.4m) deep the float is fished fixed, attached bottom only and locked in position by the bulk of the shot. Space a few light shot between the float and the hook, depending on the depth and the strength of the current.

When fishing a deeper swim, the waggler is often best fished as a slider float. In this case the bulk of the shot is placed at a depth of 8ft (2.4m), with a no. 4 shot halfway between the hook and the bulk of the shot. A no. 8 shot goes on the line about 18in. (46cm) from the hook. Tie on a stop knot at the depth of the water to ensure that the float is held at the correct depth, and this completes the tackle.

This basic rig can be used with a variety of baits in many different waters in summer when big roach are being sought. In the evening when conditions are not so bright, sweetcorn fished as a single grain on a size 14 hook, over a carpet of maggots or hemp, is most successful. Care must be taken with this method, however, for it is liable to attract large fish of other species.

Legering with a quivertip-mounted rod using bread bait is a very popular roaching method, and one that is favoured by many specimen hunters. This style is most effective for big roach in cold, wintry conditions; the

Above: *A quiet backwater of a large river will often hold a fair number of quality roach. Float fishing is best in such swims.*

Below: *A sliding float rig is used when the depth of water is deeper than the length of the rod. A stop knot prevents the float sliding too far up the line.*

bread flake is legered over mashed bread groundbait. Naturally, the same style can be used at other times of the year and with a variety of baits, but bread has been proved to be a particularly good bait during the winter months.

Swimfeeder legering can also bring excellent results. Both open and blockend feeders work well, but make a point of using small or medium-sized ones because the larger feeders, with their greater capacity, tend to attract other species.

When feeder legering in rivers in winter, use a quivertip rod with a fixed-spool reel. Add some extra weight to a small feeder so that it just holds bottom, and allow the current to form a bow in the line, producing a nice curve in the quivertip. As a fish picks up the bait it moves the feeder, which is just balanced by its weight and the tension in the line.

Bite registration appears as a slack-line movement as the quivertip springs back to the straight position. A firm strike by the angler normally results in a roach on its way to the landing net.

Below: *These two roach were taken along with a mixed catch during a night fishing session.*

RUDD *Scardinius erythrophthalmus*

Waters: Lakes, ponds, some rivers and canals.
Baits: Bread, maggots, redworms, sweetcorn, wheat.
Techniques: Float, floating crust.

Sizeable rudd are deep in the body and hump-backed. The colour runs from dark green-brown on the back, shading to a bronze or silvery bronze on the flanks, with a creamy white belly. The fins are red and the eyes are a golden red. On average they weigh 8-9oz (225-255g).

There is often confusion between the rudd and the roach, but there are external features that distinguish one from the other. The mouth of the rudd is more down-turned than that of the roach, and the dorsal fin is positioned behind the base of the pelvic fins. In the roach the dorsal is situated

Below: *The young rudd can be confused with the roach, but look for a slightly protruding lower lip. The dorsal fin is set further back than that of the roach.*

immediately above the pelvics. For certain identification the fish must be killed and dissected to allow the shape of the pharyngeal bones, or throat teeth, to be examined.

Rudd are surface and midwater feeders, so float fishing is probably the most successful method for catching them. They are usually attracted by a slow-sinking or falling bait, so the tackle should be rigged with the minimum amount of shot on the line, positioned well up from the hook to allow it and the bait to sink gently.

On rivers, trotting is often the best method and any of the usual baits may be tried. As usual, the size of hook bait selected will depend on the average size of rudd found in the water.

Groundbait or feed should consist of samples of hookbait, with the addition of a light cloudbait. Small offerings of the feed should be tossed in at the top of the swim at almost every cast, the hookbait being worked to sink with the samples.

On small lakes and ponds rudd tend to be very prolific, to the extent that

Above: *Float fishing close to a reed bed brought in this brace of specimen sized rudd.*

they overstock the water. These huge populations are invariably all stunted adults weighing 2-3oz (55-85g) each. Fishing contests held on such waters demand speed on the part of the match angler who will have to work hard to take a few pounds of very small fish.

These fish are often very easy to catch using a light float, small hook and single maggot. Big rudd of 2lb (1kg) or more are a very different proposition. When seeking these bigger fish on a large lake some time may be needed to locate a shoal. If a boat can be obtained the task will be easier, and it will enable the angler to search along the fringes of weedbeds. The shoals may not be dense, perhaps only a dozen fish, but it is possible that among them you will find one or two good specimens.

Once the shoal has been located, edge the boat cautiously into position as far from them as possible. The float tackle should be the lightest you have – a tiny peacock quill will do, with hook and bait size to match. The rudd can be induced to stay and feed by flicking in a few hookbait samples.

Although rudd feed on live insects and crustaceans, they are not generally regarded as predatory fish. However, several big specimens have been caught on small spinners cast out to lure other species of fish.

DACE *Leuciscus leuciscus*

Waters: Essentially fast running water. Streams, weirpools and gravelly runs; occasionally canals and slow rivers.
Baits: Maggots, casters, hempseed, tares, elderberries, bread, freshwater shrimp.
Techniques: Float fishing, leger, feeder-leger.

Small and delicate, the silvery dace is one of the most common of the freshwater fishes. Once known for obvious reasons as the dart, the dace is slim and very swift in its movements. When hooked on fine tackle this species puts up a fine struggle even though the average weight is no more than 6-7oz (170-200g).

In coloration the dace is predominantly silver, with a steely-blue back. The fins are usually a pale yellow, and the caudal, or tailfin, is forked. The dorsal and anal fins are concave. Sometimes an angler brings to the net what he thinks is a specimen dace, only to realise that it is a small chub. Big dace and small chub are very much alike, but the smaller species can be distinguished by the shape of the dorsal and anal fins.

Although dace are sometimes found in deep, slower rivers, they prefer the fast, shallow waters, where they frequent the clear channels between beds of streamer weed. Trout streams hold dace, but they are not encouraged in such waters because they readily take an artificial fly or nymph that has been fly-fished in the hope of catching trout.

Dace swim in shoals which keep together as they chase after food items such as flying insects and their larval forms, small crustaceans and land insects which fall into the water. A little vegetation, mostly loose pieces of weed, is also eaten.

Because it is a shoaling fish, the dace is a favourite with pleasure anglers and matchmen. An added attraction is that it will often feed in

Above right: *Dace love the fast, well-aerated waters of a weir stream such as this. These anglers are using float fishing techniques.*

Below: *The dace is a small fish, but a fighter. The concave edges of the dorsal and anal fins are important identification features.*

adverse weather and water conditions when other species do not, helping to keep a flow of fish into the keepnet.

The dace has an early spawning period, so it can be fished for throughout the coarse fishing season, provided the angler fishes his swim correctly and keeps the fish interested by feed. From mid-June, and during the summer months, many big rivers have very little flow, due perhaps to abstraction programmes and other river works. This forces the dace into the middle reaches where they can find a faster flow, which produces a higher oxygen content and, presumably, carries more food items down each hour.

To catch these fish, use a peacock waggler float, large enough to support two to three AA shots, plus a couple of no. 8 on the line. A 12ft (3.6m) carbon rod with a fixed-spool or closed-face reel, loaded with 2lb (0.9kg) b.s. line is ideal. To this add a 1lb (0.45kg) b.s. hook length and a size 18 hook.

Since the swim is likely to be in midwater, use a catapult to throw loosefeed maggots out. This is where two sturdy rod rests come in useful, as they keep the rod handle within easy reach as you use the catapult. The golden rule with this kind of fishing style is to fish only as far out as the feeder material can be thrown.

Having cast out continue to feed until bites come, then feed in smaller amounts and at regular intervals. As a guide, use a handful of maggots – about 20 to 30 – with every cast. This will keep the dace interested enough to remain in the swim.

Eventually bites will become infrequent, probably because the dace will be competing with each other for the feeder maggots, ignoring the hookbait. So try sliding the float down the line, to present the hookbait higher in the water. Different depths may have to be tried before you locate the fish again.

Plumb the swim on the line of the 'crease'. This is where the main river flow meets the slacker water, creating a visible line. When you have established the depth, slide the float down so that the hookbait hangs about 6in. (15cm) off the bottom. As before, feed the swim at almost every cast.

On many occasions dace can be caught just by letting the current take the float down the swim. Occasionally it pays to hold the float back slightly making for more direct contact when you strike. By this means better quality fish can be taken.

Dace also feed well when the river is in flood and even when the riverbanks are heavy with snow. At these times the leger style is possibly the best to use. The end tackle can be a small swimfeeder, a standard leger weight or a bomb. When legering, use a 10ft (3m) quivertip rod mounted with a fixed-spool reel loaded with 2lb (0.9kg) b.s. line. To this tie a 1lb

(0.45kg) b.s. hooklength fitted with a size 18 or 20 hook.

Even in poor conditions it is best to work the feeder tackle by casting repeatedly to a spot where the feeder will hold bottom on the minimum amount of weight. Bites in these conditions can be hard to detect and even harder to hit, so it pays to be alert and hold the rod at all times.

Right: *A catch of sizeable dace taken from a streamy swim using light float tackle.*

Below: *A fast-flowing stretch of a small, shallow river suits the dace. Float fishing a swim such as this could bring a good catch of fish.*

Hold it with one hand on the butt and rest the top joint on the front rod rest. This is comfortable, but also enables you to strike at any movement of the rod tip.

As a change from a feeder-leger, try a paternoster-type rig with a quick-release swivel. There is no need to change baits, maggot still being the best. Never forget, however, that a bait change can often bring unexpected results.

The great attraction of the dace is that it will feed when other fish are quiet. It is an obliging habit, but it is tempered by their being frustrating when they bite and hard to hook. Despite their small size they are worthy quarry for all anglers.

BLEAK *Alburnus alburnus*

Waters: Rivers, streams and occasionally canals and lakes.
Baits: Maggots, casters, hempseed, bloodworms.
Techniques: Float fishing, greased line.

This is a small, silvery fish, rarely exceeding 6in. (15cm) long. Average bleak are between 4 and 5in. (10-13cm) long, and weigh about 1oz (28g). Large bleak and small dace may be confused, but identification is possible by comparing the dorsal fins. The bleak's is convex, while that of the dace is concave. In colour the bleak is blue-green or grey-green along the back, and the sides are a brilliant silver.

The species is a useful quarry for the matchangler because the fish congregate in huge shoals swimming close to the surface, and their readiness to take a bait leads to large, possibly winning weights. Bleak are also ideal 'starter' fish for beginners. They are easy to catch on light tackle and provide great fun as they pull the hook this way and that, giving valuable practice at playing fish and handling tackle.

Being a small fish, the bleak's diet consists of plankton, surface-living insects, and insects which fall into the water, so very fine tackle is necessary: a very light rod and a reel loaded with fine nylon of about 1½lb (0.7kg) b.s. For end tackle use the smallest of floats, literally a mere matchstick or piece of peacock quill, tiny split-shot and a small hook, size 16, 18 or 20 baited with a single or double maggot. Other baits can be used, such as hemp, a fragment of bread, or bloodworm, but since they fall readily to maggots there is little point in changing baits unless the angler likes to experiment.

Regular offerings of maggots into the swim will attract bleak and draw them to within inches of the surface. If the float is then set accordingly, the bleak will throw themselves at the hookbait as soon as it hits the water.

By careful baiting up and feeding of loose maggots into the swim within easy casting distance, a shoal of bleak can be induced to stay exactly where it is wanted. In matchfishing this makes for quicker action and in consequence a heavier bag to weigh in. Some matchanglers dispense with the float and grease a short section of line. This section of the line then acts as a float and a bait indicator, its movement easily visible on the surface.

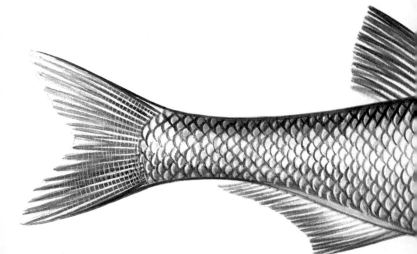

Constant casting, striking, unhooking and re-baiting at a fast rate is required for only a few pounds weight of these small fish, and for the angler who wishes to enter the matchfishing scene the practice is invaluable. If the correct tactics are employed, bleak will provide some hours of continuous, active sport, and in a competition they make a useful matchweight to back up other members of the team who may have fewer but more sizeable fish.

Some anglers make a point of fishing for bleak when they need some deadbaits for a session fishing for pike, perch, chub or zander. As deadbait, bleak can be preserved or deep-frozen and stored until required.

In the nineteenth century the scales of the bleak were used in the manufacture of artificial pearls, and they have also been caught in quantity for animal feedstuff.

Left: *A good bleak swim, such as this lock cutting, could hold a dense shoal of these small, silvery fish.*

Below: *The bleak is a good bait fish, easily caught with fine float tackle. Maximum weight is no more than 2oz (56g), though half this is average.*

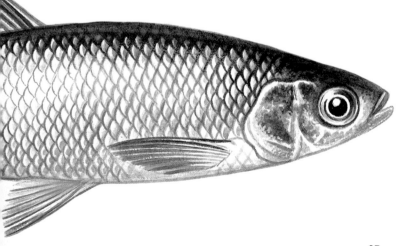

GUDGEON *Gobio gobio*

Waters: Mainly rivers and streams, occasionally canals and lakes, and enclosed waters fed by rivers.
Baits: Maggots, small worms, wheat, hemp, bread, bloodworms.
Techniques: Leger, feeder leger, float-leger, laying-on.

Gudgeon are very widely distributed throughout Britain, Europe and Asia. A member of the carp family, which also includes fish such as the bleak, roach and dace, the gudgeon is easily recognised by its shape and size. Rarely, gudgeon are mistaken for very small barbel, but this species has two pairs of barbels whereas the gudgeon has one pair. On average it weighs 1-2oz (28-55g) and is 5-6in (13-15cm) long. The coloration of the gudgeon is greyish-brown on the back, yellowish and rather blotchy on the sides and silvery on the belly. A row of spots runs along each flank.

They are bottom-living fish, which swim in small shoals and feed on insect larvae, small molluscs and crustaceans. The tiny fry eat plankton. Most shallow river swims can be expected to produce gudgeon. They prefer gravelly areas, where they gather in large numbers. Where there are shallow swims close to the bank, just away from the main flow of the river, gudgeon can congregate in huge shoals. Other likely places are laybys and lock cuttings.

It is surprising how decisive the bite of a gudgeon can be, pulling a quivertip round strongly. Many an angler has been led to believe a much more worthy fish has taken the bait. The fish is also notorious for managing to swallow baits intended for much larger fish. They are often caught unintentionally by match anglers, who accept them as part of their total weights; in fact such anglers are often very pleased to find a shoal of gudgeon in their allocated swim, for this small fish has helped many an angler into the top spot of a competition.

The best angling methods are trotting and laying-on with float tackle. Using a swim-feeder leger is often very successful, for any gudgeon in the area are quickly attracted to the offerings wriggling out of the container.

Small fish demand light tackle, both to make the sport acceptable and to present the bait properly. A small fine-wire hook is used, to suit the bait.

The best bait is the redworm. Those longer than 2in. (5cm) should be cut in two, and the hook point inserted in the cut end. Possibly the most successful bait is the bloodworm, but unless you can collect them yourself they can prove an expensive bait for such a small quarry.

The most readily obtainable bait is the ubiquitous maggot – cheap and the

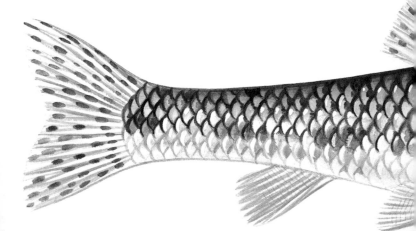

right size, even when fished singly. Whatever the hookbait, use maggots as loose feed to encourage the gudgeon to congregate. A baitdropper is the best means of placing feeder maggots on the bottom. They will not be carried so far by the current. An added attraction is cloudbait, used in conjunction with the feeder maggots.

Gudgeon are not the most exciting fish for the regular angler, but they are very useful quarry for youngsters and beginners because they are easy to catch and prolific.

Above: *Entrances to locks and similar habitats usually hold plenty of gudgeon. Bottom-living fish, they can be caught using float-leger, with light tackle.*

Below: *A small bait or beginner's fish, the gudgeon has rather a large head for its size. Groundbaiting and raking the river bottom should encourage a shoal to feed.*

GRAYLING *Thymallus thymallus*

Waters: Fast-flowing rivers and streams.
Baits: Worms, maggots, freshwater shrimps and very small fish; occasionally an artificial minnow.
Techniques: Float fishing, free-lining and fly fishing.

The grayling is a member of the salmon family, recognised by the small fleshy adipose fin near the tail, but it is classed as a coarse fish and has the same close season.

It is an attractive fish, easily recognised by its large and colourful sail-like dorsal fin. It is grey-green along the back, with irridescent or silvery flanks. There are black spots on the back and sides and a few dark zig-zag markings along the flanks.

Specimens of 3lb (1.36kg) or over are rare, the average size being below 1lb (0.45kg). It is popular with coarse anglers who regard it as a winter quarry, because it feeds at low temperatures and when other species are lying quiet.

A river fish, the grayling prefers gravelly runs through weeds and is usually found in the same waters as trout, sharing the same food. This means that some trout fisheries object to the grayling because it competes with the trout for the available food supply. It will also rise to the trout anglers' artificial flies.

The diet of the grayling is small worms, freshwater shrimps, caddis grubs, snails, insect larvae and very small fish. Like trout, they usually face upstream, lying in wait for food items that come down with the current. The bait should, therefore, be presented in this way, with the flow and as naturally as possible.

Float fishing is the most effective method, trotting small baits on light tackle. The best baits are maggots and worms. Fish the maggots two at a time on a size 14 or 16 hook. The bait has to move naturally in the current, so use a self-cocking float, with just enough shot to get the offering down, but not set too near the float. Grayling are a shoaling species, and feed in midwater, so set the float so that the bait lies clear of the bottom where it is more likely to be taken.

Use a smooth cast to place the tackle slightly upstream of the swim, tossing in a few maggots at the same time. If there are grayling there they will soon begin to feed.

Hold the float back a little so that the bait precedes it. This allows a more direct strike when the bait is

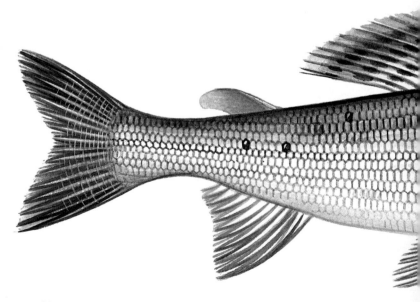

taken, resulting in a dip or some unnatural movement of the float. It may jerk sideways if the fish takes but does not dive immediately. The strike must be made in a sweep in the opposite direction to the float, to be sure of hooking the fish well.

Location of the shoal may take a while. Move slowly downstream, tossing in a few maggots at a time and watching for the splash and swirl as they are taken. Once located, hold the fish there with just a few maggots at a time while your hookbait goes to work.

Above: *Fast rivers with shallows and weedy channels suit grayling. Use light tackle so that the bait swims naturally with the current.*

Below: *The grayling has a long yet stout body and a relatively small head for its body size. It enjoys a well-oxygenated swim.*

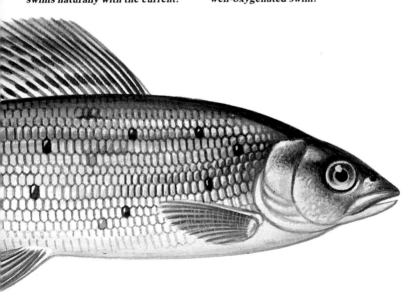

EEL *Anguilla anguilla*

Waters: All waters, running and still.
Baits: Worms, maggots, live and dead fish.
Techniques: Legering, float-leger, sink-and-draw.

The eel is unlikely to be mistaken for any other fish. Only the lamprey is similar, but this has a round, sucker-like mouth whereas the eel has proper jaws. It has a snake-like body, long and slippery, with a single pair of pectoral fins just behind the head.

Eels breed in the area of the Sargasso Sea in the Atlantic. After hatching, the young fish take some three months to reach European waters, where they enter the rivers. At this stage they are known as elvers, and are about 2½-3½in. (6-9cm) long. Elvers make useful live or dead bait for other coarse fish.

As they become adult they can grow to a considerable size. Fish of over 10lb (4.5kg) have been caught on rod and line. When mature they are dark greenish-brown on the back, shading to yellow underneath. This alters as the eel migrates back to the sea to breed – the yellow becomes silvery and complex internal changes take

place to enable it to live in salt water.

In rivers, eels prefer the slow-flowing reaches, staying among the roots of weedbeds. Where they live in lakes they become more plentiful and larger, and often remain for long periods buried in the mud.

Eels feed on almost every kind of aquatic creature, including fish, so any of the ordinary baits can be used. An average-sized eel can be caught on a big worm such as a lob, or a bunch of smaller worms such as brandlings. For big eels the best bait is a dead fish such as a dace or a gudgeon – although a sprat has been the downfall of eels of 6-9lb (2.7-4kg). For long-casting, the deadbait is mounted on a large hook, single or treble, by using a baiting needle to thread the trace through the body of the fish from tail to mouth.

Having cast out, use rod rests and attach bite indicators. Then wait patiently for a take. Eels feed at any time of day or night, and legering is the most effective method of seeking them out deliberately.

Big eels are powerful fish, and it is wise to have a few traces prepared ready for use. At the top of the line, fit a link-swivel for easy attachment to

Below: The eel's only true fins are the pectorals. The remnants of earlier fins can now be seen as a fringe on the back and underside of the body.

the trace. When a large, writing eel is caught the trace can be detached at once and a fresh bait and trace connected for recasting. The old trace and hook can be removed from the eel later – even at home, if the fish is taken back to be eaten.

Although the eel has scales, it exudes a thick covering of slimy mucus which disguises the scales when it is picked up. This slime makes it very difficult to hold the fish while the hook is removed. A sure way to

Above: *A fully grown eel is a powerful fish. Widely distributed, eels are found in all types of waters, and will even undertake short overland journeys if necessary to reach a favoured stretch of landlocked water.*

keep the writing eel still is to lay it on a sheet of newspaper, where it will lie quietly, probably because the sticky adhesive effect of the mucus discourages movement.

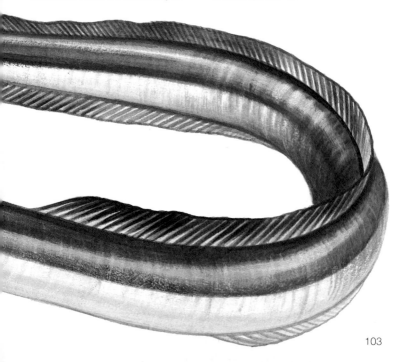

PIKE *Esox lucius*

Waters: Reservoirs, lakes, ponds, gravel pits, canals, rivers and streams.
Baits: Live and dead fish, crayfish, lobworms, spinners and plugs.
Techniques: Float fishing, legering, paternoster, sink and draw, spinning.

One of the commonest coarse fishes, the pike is a vicious predator, with a huge mouth equipped with sharp, backward-pointing teeth. It can grow very big, and specimens of 40-50lb (18-23kg) are on record; many weighing 20lb (9kg) and over are taken every season.

The pike has a large head which accounts for about a quarter of its total body length. Its snout is shaped like a duck's bill, the lower jaw projecting. It has a long, slim body with rounded anal and dorsal fins situated close to the tailfin; its pelvic fins are about halfway along the body, and its pectorals are close to the head. It is dark greenish-brown along the back, and pale green on the sides with creamy white blotches forming curved patterns. The underside is a creamy yellow.

It is difficult to confuse the pike with any other species, the only fish having any resemblance to it being the zander. There is no direct relationship between them, however, even though the zander has been given the name of pike-perch. The zander is a distinct species quite unrelated to either the pike or the perch.

Although pike are essentially fish eaters, predating on any small fish – including the young of their own species – they will also feed on various other creatures that swim on, or fall into the water. They have been known to take animals as large as ducks from the surface.

Like perch, pike can be located by the sudden scattering of small fish on the surface. Anglers fishing for roach and dace regularly have their hooked fish snatched off the line by a marauding pike.

During recent years pike have become increasingly popular with anglers, one of the main reasons being their availability. Practically every coarse fisherman lives within easy travelling range of a good pike fishery. Many kinds of water, even farm ponds, have a head of pike present, and some of these fish may grow to an exceptional size if they have lived there for some years and there are plenty of small food-fish present. Even half-acre sand pits have produced fish weighing nearly 30lb (13.6kg), sometimes to the astonishment of the angler.

The principal bait for pike is fish, dead or alive. On rivers and canals, livebaits work better than deadbaits. A common technique with a large livebait is to suspend it from a big spherical float known as a bung. A sliding pilot float is threaded on to the line above the bung; when a pike runs

with the bait and drags the bung under, the pilot float slides up the line and stays on the surface to give the angler an indication of the pike's movements. Some anglers prefer to keep the livebait small and fish it on a float-paternoster rig, using a streamlined slider float to support the bait as it swims around.

For the increasing number of anglers who do not like the idea of using a live fish as bait, spinning is an attractive and often productive alternative. Lures of all kinds can also be used. Plugs of the slow-sinking variety are very popular, as are copper-coloured spoons – copper for some reason being a highly attractive colour to a feeding pike. Spinning is the one method that can be used to

Above: *A weighty pike, hooked in a quiet pool of a small river, is drawn ever closer to a large landing net held at the ready.*

Below: *The pike is built for hunting. Its lean, elongated body and swept-back fins allow it the necessary speed to catch its prey.*

Above: *This 30 lb (13.6 kg) pike fell to a livebait, float-fished in a large, shallow natural lake.*

good effect on all types of pike water, but it must be stressed that artificial lures tend to catch only small to medium-sized pike.

On stillwaters, deadbait fishing is without doubt the most efficient technique. Deadbaits have many advantages. They are easy to obtain, simple to keep and use, and they save a great deal of valuable fishing time. They also tend to lure large pike more consistently than any of the other common pike baits.

The choice of fish for deadbait is endless. A visit to the local fishmonger will yield a plentiful supply of sprats, sardines, herrings, mackerel and even smelt. Of these, sardine and mackerel have caught more large pike than the others. A sardine is oily and attracts pike both by smell and by the flash of its silvery body. Mackerel is also oily, and its streamlined shape and weight allows it to be cast further than most deadbaits. On heavily fished waters where pike tend to shun the banks, mackerel hookbait can be fished outside the normal casting range, where it is often most effective.

Where to fish for pike varies from water to water. In rivers, the fish tend to seek out the slack areas. Once they start feeding, however, pike will vacate the slacks and eddies and move out into the faster, shallower water in search of prey fish.

Below: *Spinning allows the angler to search a wider area, casting into all the likely places. Give the rod a little flick occasionally to make the lure dart like a small fish.*

In stillwaters, pike can usually be found on drop-offs – places where the bottom falls away steeply into deep water. Surface and sunken weedbeds can also be productive, as can the points of an island or submerged gravel bars.

The selection of tackle for pike fishing is never easy. For livebaiting or deadbaiting, an 11-12ft (3.3 3.7m) rod is best. For spinning, the general preference is for a 10ft (3m) rod. Rods for casting baits should have a test-curve of over 2lb (0.9kg), depending on the size of bait to be cast, whereas a test-curve of 1½lb (0.7kg) is ample for a spinning rod.

Most pike anglers use fixed-spool reels. Make sure, however, that the spool is large enough to hold at least

Below: *While the pike's body is supported in the net, two fingers hooked in the gill covers immobilise the fish while the hook is removed using artery forceps.*

150yd (137m) of 12-15lb (5.4-6.8kg) b.s. line. The spool should also be wide and shallow enough to make long casting easy.

Pike tackle need not be expensive. For live or deadbait fishing there is little point in purchasing the expensive carbon or boron rods. Fibreglass is perfectly adequate since the rods spend most of their time sitting on the rod rests and weight therefore is of little consideration. Lightweight spinning rods are to be preferred, however, because they are held all the time.

These days, most pike anglers use barbless hooks. They have many advantages over the old trebles with their huge barbs. A fish hooked on a barbless hook is easy to free, allowing it to be weighed, photographed and released to the water quickly, almost unharmed. Anglers are now actively conserving pike and the barbless treble has become an essential part of the pike angler's equipment.

PERCH *Perca fluviatilis*

Waters: Rivers, canals, reservoirs, lakes, ponds.
Baits: Worms, maggots, small live fish such as minnow or gudgeon. Artificial lures, small plugs and spinners.
Techniques: Spinning, float fishing, legering, paternostering.

There is no doubt that the perch is one of the most handsome of our freshwater fishes. It is deep-bodied, and slightly hog-backed. There are two separate dorsal fins, the first with sharp spines, the second with soft rays supported at each end by spines.

The general coloration of the perch is a dark olive-green along the back, shading through golden-yellow on the flanks, to white or silver on the belly. The pelvic and ventral fins are tinged with red. When the fish is in prime condition, and at spawning time, the dark vertical bars on the flanks are very distinctive.

The perch is a predator, which feeds on any small fish it can catch. It likes to lie in ambush for its prey, keeping in submerged roots, weedbeds, supports of bridges and piles, indeed any obstruction that offers cover. From here it makes fierce attacks on small passing fish. In winter it can often be detected by the sudden surface panic of a shoal of small fish as a perch comes marauding from its hiding place.

The predatory nature of the perch makes it susceptible to a moving bait, so spinning with small flashy lures can produce some larger-than-average specimens, in the 3lb (1.36kg) class. You should work the spinning lure or plug along the fringe of a weedbed, across the mouth of a tributary, or close to likely hiding places. Keep the spinner moving well, but constantly vary the depth, for the perch will be attracted by an apparently ailing fish moving erratically through the water.

To take perch on a bait, cast a lobworm or small fish into the swim, using a float to present the bait at about mid-water level. The size of the float will depend upon wind and water conditions. It pays to keep the bait on the move by recasting, and vary the depth of the bait by moving the float up and down the line.

A redworm, hooked once in the middle to leave both ends free to wriggle, also makes a good perch bait; it will attract any perch in the immediate vicinity. Small perch can be taken on maggots trotted down in the river current.

Perch of average size stay in shoals. When such a shoal is found it is fairly easy to hold the fish with feeder particles while float fishing a maggot hookbait. A fair number can be taken this way. If the takes dwindle, it can occasionally pay to switch to a worm bait, fishing this through the swim. The shoal may have a hefty specimen

hanging round the fringe, and a large lob may tempt a big fish where the smaller maggots fail.

The paternoster can be effective if an area of lake needs to be searched systematically. One of the main advantages in using this method is that a bait can be presented just where it is required, and held there if need be. When paternostering, worms and small fish on a size 8 or 6 hook should be used as bait.

For really long casting, switch to a basic leger rig. It usually comes into its own when lake fishing, for rivers are rarely as wide as lakes. Big perch can lurk round known weedbeds well out in pits or lakes, and a large lob is the best bait to entice them to bite.

Below: *The perch has a spiny front dorsal which bristles defiantly when it is in danger or under stress. This makes it advisable to use a net when handling the fish.*

ZANDER *Stizostedion luciiperca*

Waters: Lakes, canals, drains and slow-moving rivers.
Baits: Small fish such as minnows, bleak, gudgeon and other small cyprinids, and lobworms.
Techniques: Float fishing, legering, paternoster, free-lining, spinning.

The zander is also known as the pike-perch, but despite this it is not a hybrid but a distinct species. An attractive fish, it has a long, slim body, with silver to greenish-gold on the sides, merging into a silvery-white belly. The back is greenish-grey, and there are two speckled dorsal fins, the first spiny, the second with soft rays. It can reach quite weighty proportions, possibly over 20lb (9kg), but fish of near that weight are rare.

The fish is a nocturnal predator on all fish when adult, zander fry feeding on insects and crustaceans. The larger specimens are often solitary. Spawning activity occurs between April and June.

While small zander are usually found near the bottom, bigger ones can be caught almost anywhere on a water, but being predators they will always be in the vicinity of a shoal of small fish. To catch zander the angler should rove the bank, searching all the likely places until the fish are located. Each area should be fished for about 30 minutes before moving to another spot perhaps 20yd (18m) further on.

Once found, a shoal of zander will offer exciting sport, but they will all be of average to small size. They can be attracted into a swim or induced to feed by groundbaiting with chopped or minced fish. The best hookbait is a small fish, presented live on float or paternoster tackle.

For float fishing, use a rod of about 11ft (3.4m), with a centrepin or fixed-spool reel. The terminal tackle should include the lightest float that supports the bait. For a livebait, the ideal float is one that the fish can tow but not pull under. The bait should be mounted on size 8 or 10 trebles, one or two on a fine-wire trace or substantial nylon. Some anglers prefer a wire trace in case a pike takes the bait, bites through the nylon, and swims off with trebles embedded in its jaws.

Legering is ideal for long-range fishing and deep swims. The rod should be about 10-11ft (3-3.4m), preferably fitted with interchangeable quivertips. Bites can also be registered by a bobbin or some form of bite indicator on the line. The fixed-spool reel allows longer casting. Load it with

8 or 10lb (3.6-4.5kg) b.s. line depending on the water. Select the lightest free-running weight that can be used effectively. For this style, a single size 6 hook is preferred and the bait can be lobworm or deadbait for long casting.

Take care when removing the hooks, for zander have long sharp teeth which can cause painful wounds.

Some water authorities and angling associations have banned the zander from waters they control. This means that illegal stocking with the species can lead to prosecution. Anglers are also expected to remove any zander they catch from certain waters. Fishermen who like zander fishing must respect these rules, but there is a bonus in that the fish is good to eat.

Above: *This handsome specimen of zander, in excellent condition, was caught on a small livebait, float-fished in a sluggish river.*

Below: *The zander is a sleek, predatory fish with a large, tooth-filled mouth. It may be encountered in a wide variety of waters.*

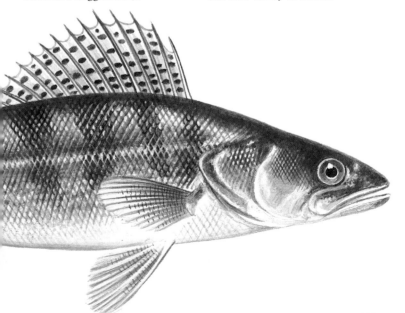

WELS *Silurus glanis*

Waters: Lakes, reservoirs, canals, rivers.
Baits: Worms, luncheonmeat, dead fish.
Techniques: Various leger and float-leger styles.

The wels, or catfish, is not often taken in Britain, for it has a restricted distribution, being confined to waters in Bedfordshire and Buckinghamshire to which it was introduced from the European Continent. In Europe it is common in lakes and rivers in Russia, southern Sweden, Germany and so on, and was particularly associated with the Danube basin, receiving the name Danubian wels in consequence.

The wels prefers sluggish waters, muddy lakes and the deep pools of large rivers. Like all the catfish family, it has barbels round its wide mouth. The head is broad and the back smooth, apart from a small dorsal fin near the head. A very long anal fin runs back to the tail. Coloration is drab, with a greenish-brown back, shading to a mottled yellow-brown on the flanks and a pale cream belly. Sometimes the back is a sooty dark grey, mottled with yellow.

This fish can grow to enormous size, with authenticated weights of 500lb (227kg) from eastern Europe. Since so few are caught in Britain it is difficult to give an average weight, but any wels over 30lb (13.6kg) is considered a large specimen. It is thought that wels of at least 70lb (32kg) exist in English waters.

In fishing terms the wels is a most exciting fish. Many very large specimens have been hooked by big-fish specialists who are used to grappling with this ponderous yet powerful creature.

Any angler hoping to tangle with a wels must be armed with high-powered tackle. A 10-11ft (3-3.3m) rod with a strong, reliable fixed-spool reel holding at least 150 yards (137m) of 15lb (6.8kg) b.s. line provides the basics. A large landing net will be needed to safely engulf a large wels, one with a 3ft (1m) diameter carp net and a bag about 4ft (3.6m) deep.

Wels tend to be most active in the summer, when shallow stillwaters are at their warmest, although these fish have been tempted well into October when an Indian summer has stretched beyond the usual period. They feed by day and by night, and if the regulations of the water permit it, night fishing is probably the favourite time, one reason being that it will be quieter. The half-dozen 6in. (15cm) barbels round the fish's mouth will pick up the smallest bankside vibration, sending the fish back into the security of the depths.

The most common fishing style is simple – no rig at all, just a strong size 2 or 4 hook, depending on bait size, tied free-line fashion direct to the reel line. The eye of the wels is small, so it is not surprising that it hunts for food

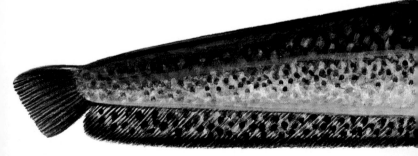

mainly by smell and 'feel' using its barbels. Its natural food is small fish – alive or dead – and to these baits the angler can add small pieces of squid, bunches of lobworms, or a variety of 'cocktail' specials.

Heavy prebaiting or groundbaiting probably has more drawbacks than advantages, so once the baited hook is cast out fishing is simply a waiting game, often long and uneventful! But when that line begins to twitch and then hiss from the open spool the fun and skill really begin. Great care should be taken when playing the fish. If it is a really big wels do not bully it or hurry it. The fight can last half an

Above: *It takes two anglers to hold a big, lively wels. This specimen weighed in at a very respectable 43½ lb (19.7 kg).*

hour, and if you have a reliable friend take advantage of that spare pair of hands – they will be needed when you get the angry thrashing monster to the landing net.

Below: *Not a fish many people would call attractive, the wels has a broad head, wide mouth with very long barbels, and a long tapering body. The skin of the wels is quite scaleless.*

INDEX

USEFUL ADDRESSES

Water Authorities

Anglian Water Authority, Ambury Road, Huntingdon PE18 6NZ
Telephone: 0480 56181

Northumbrian Water Authority, Northumbria House, Regent Centre, Gosforth,
Newcastle upon Tyne NE3 3PX
Telephone: 0632 843151

North West Water Authority, Dawson House, Gt Sankey, Warrington WA5 3LW
Telephone: 092 572 4321

Severn-Trent Water Authority, Abelson House, 2297 Coventry Road, Sheldon,
Bimingham B26 3PR
Telephone: 021 743 4222

Southern Water Authority, Guildbourne House, Chatsworth Road, Worthing,
Sussex
Telephone: 0903 205252

South West Water Authority, Penninsula House, Rydon Lane, Exeter EX2 7HR
Telephone: 0392 33160

Thames Water Authority, Nugent House, Vastern Road, Reading,
Berks RG1 8DB
Telephone: 0734 593538

Welsh Water Authority, Cambrian Way, Brecon, Powys LD3 7HP
Telephone: 0874 3181

Wessex Water Authority, (Fisheries & Recreation Dept), P.O. Box 9,
Kings Square, Bridgwater, Somerset TA6 2EA
Telephone: 0278 57333

Yorkshire Water Authority, West Riding House, 67 Albion Street,
Leeds LS1 5AA
Telephone: 0532 44820

Commercial Fisheries

Amey Anglers Association, ARC, Administrative Office, Besselsleigh Road,
Abingdon
Telephone: 0865 730851

Leisure Sport Angling, (Manager), Thorpe Park, Staines Road, Chertsey, Surrey
KT16 8PN
Telephone: 093 28 64872

Redland Angling Scheme, Lakeview Farm, Old Bury Hill, Dorking, Surrey
Telephone: 0306 883621

William Boyer Fishing, (Fishery Manager), Trout Road, West Drayton,
Middlesex
Telephone: 0895 444707

Specialist Clubs and Associations

Anglers Co-operative Association, Midland Bank Chambers, Westgate,
Grantham, Lincs NG31 6LE
Telephone: 0476 61008

Birmingham Anglers Association, 100 Icknield Port Road, Birmingham B16 0AP
Telephone: 021 454 9111

British Carp Study Group, Newhaven, Marsh Lane, Easton-in-Gordano,
Bristol BS20 0NH

British Casting Association, 'Eskdale', 2 Janmead, Hutton, Brentwood, Essex

British Field Sports Society, 59 Kennington Road, London SE1 7PZ

British Naturalists' Association, 6 Chancery Place, The Green, Writtle,
Essex CM1 3DY

British Record (rod-caught) Fish Committee, 11 Cowgate,
Peterborough PE1 1LZ
Telephone: 0733 54084

British Trust for Conservation Volunteers, 36 St Mary's Street, Wallingford,
Oxfordshire OX10 0EU

British Waterways Board, Melbury House, Melbury Terrace,
London NW1 6JX

Carp Anglers' Association, Heywood House, Pill, Bristol BS20 OEA

Carp Society, 4 South Hanningfield Way, Runwell, Wickford, Essex

Catfish Conservation group, 13 Bowyers Mews, Neath Hill,
Milton Keynes MK14 6HP

Central Association of London & Provincial Angling Clubs, Secretary, 9 Kemble
Road, Croydon, Surrey

Council for Environmental Conservation, Zoological Gardens, Regent's Park,
London NW1 4RY

The Field Studies Council, Information Office, Preston Montford, Montford
Bridge, Shrewsbury SY4 1HW

Freshwater Biological Association, Ferry House, Far Sawry, Ambleside,
Cumbria LA22 0LP

Freshwater Fisheries Group, Dept of Zoology, P.O. Box 147, Brownlow Street,
Liverpool L69 3BX

Inland Waterways Association, 114 Regent's Park Road, London NW1 8UQ

Continued over page

Institute of Fisheries Management, 'Balmaha', Coldwells Road, Holmer,
Hereford

John Eastwood Water Protection Trust, Alverstoke, Greenway Lane,
Bath BA2 4LN

London Anglers' Association, Forest Road Hall, Hervey Park Road,
Walthamstow, London E17 3AP
Telephone: 01 520 7477

National Anguilla Club, 6 Ludlow Drive, Stritchley, Telford, Shropshire

National Anglers Council, 11 Cowgate, Peterborough PE1 1LZ
Telephone 0733 54084

National Association of Specialist Anglers, 5 Delamare Road, Meadow Rise,
Bewdley, Worcs

National Federation of Anglers, Halliday House, 2 Wilson Street, Derby DE1
1PG

Nature Conservancy Council, 19-20 Belgrave Square, London SW1X 8PY

The Pike Society, 10 Brittania Road, Norwich, Norfolk NR1 4HP

Pure Rivers Society, Secretary, 74 Dagenham Avenue, Dagenham, Essex

Royal Society for Nature Conservation, The Green, Nettleham,
Lincoln LN2 2NR

Sports Council, 16 Upper Woburn Place, London WC1

Sussex County Anglers' Association, Secretary, The Bungalow, Lingfield, Sussex

The Tenchfishers, 21 Ashdown Close, Chandlers Ford, Hants SO5 1QF

Underwater Association, Dept of Zoology, University of Bristol, Woodland
Road, Bristol BS8 1UG

PICTURE CREDITS

Artists
Copyright of the artwork illustrations on the pages following the artists' names is
the property of Salamander Books Ltd.

Colin Newman (Linden Artists): 18, 20, 21, 22, 28, 29, 30, 37, 38, 44, 49, 50-51,
52-53, 53 (top), 54, 55 (both), 57 (both), 59, 61, 80, 81, 84, 88, 106
Eric Tenney: 66-67, 70-71, 74-75, 78-79, 82-83, 86-87, 90-91, 92-93, 96-97,
98-99, 100-101, 102-103, 104-105, 108-109, 110-111, 112-113, Back cover

Photographs
All the photographs in this book are by Bill Howes with the exception of the
following:
Frank Gutfield: 113
Shakespeare Company: 14 (top), 15
John Wilson: 42, 43, 76, 89, 107